Confident Public Speaking

How to design and deliver an enjoyable an informative presentation

Paddy Spruce

Published 2021

Copyright. Paddy Spruce 2021

Author contact: paddy@paddyspruce.com.au

Website: www. paddyspruce.com.au

ISBN: 978-0-6450947-0-1

All rights reserved. No part of this publication may be reproduced, stored in a retrieval system or transmitted in any form by any means, electronic, mechanical, photocopying, recording or otherwise, without the prior written permission of the publishers and copyright holder.

Paddy Spruce asserts the moral right to be identified as the author of this work.

Acknowledgements

I have had so much help from so many people in writing this book or becoming the person who wrote this book.

Three people stand out as being instrumental in getting the book finished. The first is Dr. Russ Harris. Russ is a doctor, author, psychotherapist and a friend. His advice and support have been invaluable. He is a true expert in Mindfulness and ACT which is the psychotherapeutic application of mindfulness.

The second person is David Brewster. David is a professional ghost writer and photographer. David has encouraged and assisted me to complete this book. He is a generous friend, encourager and non-judgmental listener. David is an ideal person to bounce ideas off and is one of the most reliable people I know.

The third person is my beautiful wife Hilary who supports me in everything I do. Her constant love makes everything seem easy.

I am truly blessed to have her in my life.

Paddy Spruce

Chapters

Getting started

1. Confident Public Speaking
2. Fear and other myths
3. Opening
4. The body
5. The close
6. Memorable Information
7. Visual support
8. The famous five mistakes
9. Mindful listening
10. Script or impromptu?
11. Trouble shooting
12. Hit the road
13. Dessert
14. Personality and other excuses
15. Next level
16. Keep reading

Appendices

Getting Started

Have you ever stood up to speak and...your voice sat down?

Have you ever felt the need to speak out but thought you might leave it until next time? I certainly have. Many times.

This book will help you find your message...and your voice.

We all have a message. We all have a voice. Sometimes we forget our message or lose our voice. Your message is what you want to say. Your voice is how you say it. Let's combine the two and call them speaking. There are times when we must speak and let others know our message.

Maybe you are unsure about what to speak about or find it hard to speak up when the need arises.

The aim of this book is to help you find your message or topic and also to live with and manage the unhelpful thoughts that inhibit your performance when speaking in public.

So, this is a book about speaking…. confidently and mindfully.

Speaking is something we all do throughout the day. Call it public speaking and many people shrink. All speaking is public speaking really unless you speak to yourself. Usually this is not aloud or allowed.

I have combined Public Speaking with Mindfulness, a perfect marriage. Speaking is finding your message and your voice and Mindfulness is the key to staying focused and calm … and avoiding dying while you are speaking which is very unlikely except in your imagination.

The best way I know of handling speaker's nerves is to be fully present and let disturbing thoughts drift by without engaging them. Do what you are doing with all your attention. Getting rid of your nerves even sounds silly, don't you think? Why get rid of them if they are there to help you.

Your thoughts are never the problem. It's your engagement with these thoughts that creates a problem. The same for your feelings. They are not the problem. Attempting to avoid unhelpful feelings or paying them too much attention is the problem.

Rosa Parks started the civil rights revolution by simply saying "No" when asked to give her seat to another person on a bus. In 1955, she was seated in the section for African Americans. It was usual practice for African Americans to give up their seats for white passengers when the white section was full. The bus driver told Rosa to give up her seat and she said "NO".

A simple message and a determined voice that was heard around the world. It started the civil rights movement in the USA and launched the career of Martin Luther King.

She found her voice and had the courage to use it. I don't know for sure but she probably had thoughts that would have made it hard for her to speak out. She probably also had feelings that made it very difficult for her to refuse to give up her seat.

Malala Yousafzai also spoke out and continues to do so despite being shot for expressing her views about the need to educate young women. As a fifteen-year-old girl you can be sure she was hindered by fearful thoughts.

As Rosa Parks had done before her, Malala found her voice too. She was just fifteen when she was shot in the face by a cowardly assassin. It is unlikely that she is fearless each time she speaks about the need to educate young girls. She knew her life was in danger. It still is. She must have felt anxious. She continues anyway. She seems calm. She acts calmly despite unhelpful thoughts.

If you are reading this, I assume that you want to improve your public speaking and presenting to a group larger than one.

I have often asked people how many people in an audience make them nervous and the number varies from a few to hundreds. Strangely, some have a specific number. OK with five but nervous with ten. OK with fifty but nervous with one hundred.

My suggestion to get most from this book is to read each chapter slowly more than once and then do the exercises for at least a week. This will develop skill. The theory is easy to grasp. The skill comes with hard work. You knew this, already didn't you?

Also examine your mental attitude. Many people reject public speaking because of nerves. You will get more from reading this book if you move past this 'reject' mode. Move at least to 'accept' mode. Trying to improve your speaking while in reject mode makes the job so much harder. It is like driving with the handbrake on. In accept mode you use your energy to improve. It may be tough but the effort will help you for the rest of your life. Be kind to yourself. Focus on improving. Look for help and support.

You have a voice. Use it with groups of any size. It's the same speaking for any sized group. Fear often deludes us into thinking that group size matters. It doesn't. This book will help you see past this delusion. Imagine being in the dark. Would you worry about the size of the audience? If you are being interviewed on the radio, does it matter how many people are listening? Same message, same words, same answers.

I remember having mixed feelings about a speaking engagement in Dublin. I was excited to be asked to speak at an overseas conference. I was a little worried about speaking in a place I had never visited before, to a foreign audience. I now know that this anxiety is normal and commonplace. It goes with the territory.

It took me a while to recognise that the unhelpful thoughts were outside my control. What I could control was whether I engaged them or let them pass. I slowly got to acceptance.

The stage after acceptance is enjoyment. You can come to enjoy speaking. I do and so do many of my colleagues who are speakers. I am a founding member of the National Speakers Association in Victoria, now Professional Speakers Australia, and many of my friends speak about how much they enjoy speaking to make a difference and to make a good living.

Once you enjoy speaking, you will look for and create opportunities instead of accepting them when offered. You don't have to wait for this enjoyment to arrive. You can do an excellent job in the acceptance mode.

I now really enjoy speaking at an overseas conference.

So, start reading with an attitude of acceptance and a readiness for hard work. Be open to the possibility that you might come to enjoy public speaking. As you improve, you will seem different from the majority who would rather die than speak in public according to many surveys. People don't die from speaking. Let me know if you see someone die from speaking in public.

Developing mindfulness techniques will help your speaking and your enjoyment of life.

So, what is mindfulness?

In his book 'The Confidence Gap', Dr Russ Harris calls mindfulness a mental state of awareness, openness and focus. When we are mindful, we engage in what we are doing, let go of unhelpful thoughts and take action without being distracted by our emotions.

The three key mindfulness skills are defusion, expansion and engagement.

Defusion is the ability to separate from your thoughts instead of getting caught up in them.

Expansion is the ability to make room for emotions and let them come and go.

Engagement is the ability to be fully aware of what is happening in the present.

I will elaborate further in this book.

Do the exercises at the end of each chapter until you have got a good hold of the skills. Practise mindfulness until it becomes second nature.

The exercises may feel unnatural for a while. It won't feel like you. Eventually they will feel natural. Your hard work will lead to wonderful benefits. You will become a new you, a more skilled you. Actually, <u>you</u> won't change but your effectiveness as a speaker will.

Approach speaking and presenting as if you can't fail. If success is continuing to improve then as long as you are improving you are succeeding. Take your time to master the skills and change your attitude. Be very kind to yourself. Keep trying until you do improve. Thomas Edison was famous for finding out how not to make electric light bulbs … until he found a successful method.

Our minds will want to compare us to others who are better or worse than us. The meaningful comparison is you then with you now.

So, I will cover all aspects of designing and delivering an effective presentation or speech as well as managing your unhelpful thoughts.

Good luck on the journey of enjoyable speaking. It really is a journey rather than a destination as you will keep changing and improving. You won't arrive at speaking success. Success is really a verb although it looks like a noun. Don't go back to normal. Move forward to a new normal.

I know the journey metaphor has been done to death but

Bon Voyage anyway.

Your first exercise is to decide whether you want to master the skill of public speaking and whether you want to move from rejecting or avoiding speaking to accepting opportunities when offered to you.

If you really do want to go down the speaking path, make a deal with yourself now to keep at it until you see a speaking opportunity as a challenge. A challenge always has an element of risk but once accepted, the risk is seen as a part of the package. The flip side of the challenge coin is fear. No fear. No challenge.

This may sound strange but humour me and help yourself.

Write down words you would like to use to describe yourself as a speaker. What values matter to you?

Complete this sentence.

As a speaker, I want to embody …

Do you want to embody these qualities or values when you feel relaxed? What happens when you don't feel relaxed? Do you want to live and demonstrate these qualities whether you feel relaxed or anxious? I do.

You may not able to control your thoughts and feelings but you can choose the values and qualities you focus on when speaking in public.

What values matter to you?

A simple mindfulness technique is to recognise unhelpful thoughts as the imposters they are and let them pass by like the cars that drive by when you are enjoying your coffee at a footpath café.

Enjoy your coffee and let the cars pass hardly noticed.

Try this exercise. Imagine yourself agreeing to speak to an audience larger than what is comfortable for you. Let's say that you are asked, at the last moment, to fill in for a speaker at a business meeting or conference. You know the topic but not as well as some in the audience.

What thoughts come to mind? How do you feel once the implications hit home?

Imagine you have a waiting room for these thoughts. They take a number from the receptionist and sit down. You let them wait as you are busy doing another job. Some leave after a short wait. Some wait longer. Some stay a long time. Practise letting them linger in the waiting room. The receptionist won't let them into your office until you give permission.

Stay in the present and let them wait in the background. Focus on what you are doing. Don't try to get rid of the thoughts. Make sure they have enough room.

I have been in this situation many times especially when speaking to an audience in a foreign country. Sometimes my mind says things like " The person in the front row is unhappy with something you just said" or "I left out something that I wanted to say but I am now running out of time" or "Why did I agree to speak to this audience?"

My worst experience was when a man in the front row started reading a newspaper. Foolishly, I spoke to him and said "Looks like you would rather read the paper than listen to me." I can't print what he said to me.

I should have just got on with my presentation and left him in the waiting room instead of inviting him into my office or giving him the microphone.

In the following chapters I will cover these important topics:

How to manage your fear of speaking – your 'nerves'.

The opening – How to get off to a good start.

The body – How to cut your message into bite size pieces

The close - How to create an inspiring close

How to make your information memorable and sticky.

Visual support How to use pictures to reinforce your message.

How to recognise mistakes and avoid them.

Read on and practise on.

Remember, if you can speak to one person, you can speak to many.

Decide whether you want to develop your speaking skills and are willing to do the necessary hard work.

The steps will sound simple but they are not easy.

Get started now!

2. Fear and other myths

I mentioned that I was asked to speak in Dublin, early in my speaking career.

I remember the telephone call from a man with a warm Irish accent asking whether I was interested to speak at a conference in Dublin in two months' time.

Initially I thought it was a friend having a lend of me as I thought I could recognise his voice despite the accent. I soon realised that it was a genuine enquiry and agreed to speak. It was for a group of English removalists. After agreeing, I spoke to a friend who had spoken at the same conference the previous year. She told me they were a very tough audience and that the conference was more of a junket than a legitimate conference. I now started to feel uncomfortable. My mind bothered me with thoughts like "Why didn't I call my colleague before agreeing?"

I had two months to prepare and did it tough. I really was plagued with negative thoughts all the way to Dublin. I had to work hard not to ruminate. They were a very tough audience and it was a junket for them and a very valuable learning experience for me.

Does fear prevent you from doing something you really want to do? Does it prevent you from speaking at a meeting? Does it make your preparation more difficult than necessary?

If you were able to live with your fear instead of letting it hold you back, what would you do?

In my three decades of helping people develop their speaking skills, the most frequent stated need is 'More confidence.' This usually means less fear.

I remember hearing a speaker ask an audience member this question "Who and what do you focus on when you are speaking?" The person answered, "I focus on myself and how I am feeling?" The speaker suggested that this was the root of the problem of nerves and offered a simple solution. "Why not try focusing on your audience, their needs and how they are feeling?"

Focusing on unhelpful thoughts that lead to fear is a major hindrance to deal with if you want to become a calm, confident speaker.

Fear is essential for survival. It can prevent us from thinking clearly if we make it our focus. Many, many years ago, our ancestors lived in constant fear for their lives. Either that or they got angry and tried to defend themselves. Their existence was threatened by animals that didn't take so long to mature and had much bigger teeth. They looked for food and protected themselves most of the day and night. I don't think they had time to ponder the meaning of their lives.

Modern man and woman have moved into a different world with the same brain or at least a very similar one. We have a very strong reaction to a fearful situation like a dog attack or…a request to speak to an audience. We can have an identical reaction to these very different situations.

I remember attending a full day defensive driving course at a race track.

I clearly remember thinking that I would slide on the corners and roll the car. I gripped the steering wheel very tightly. As I did more laps, I gradually listened to the instructor and focused on what I was being told. I let the scary thoughts go and focused on the helpful advice I was being given. I now started to enjoy the fast laps. I held the wheel loosely.

It is nearly impossible to be creative or speak impromptu when in survival mode. Parts of your brain shut down. You can hardly enjoy public speaking if your body is stressed and producing a flood of cortisol.

Managing your fear and anxiety is the first step to becoming an accomplished speaker who enjoys the opportunity to inform and move an audience. Mastery sounds great but I really encourage you to speak with fear rather than aim to master, conquer or get rid of it. How can you conquer your own feelings? Better to accept and live with them. Fearless is like driving with your traction control switched off in the rain. You have turned off technology that is meant to help you. Fear is also meant to help you. Fear is good. It warns you. It is not meant to disable you.

Anxiety and fear are very common responses to being asked to speak to an audience. Rather than get rid of or combat these feelings, make room for them and treat them as guests. Guests who want to help you. They want to protect and warn you. They don't want you to stop altogether. Eventually you will learn to live with them and hardly notice that they are present. The guests you feed will return. Do you want them to return? If not, don't give them attention or feed them.

I often feel uncomfortable just before a presentation and my mind produces thoughts like…

Have I prepared well enough?

What if they already know what I am speaking about?

What if there is someone in the audience who knows a lot more about the topic than I do?

What if I get a question that I can't answer?

I am getting much better at recognising these as merely thoughts and letting them pass.

Haven't you ever had someone home for dinner and found them annoying or boring? You may have wanted them to leave but they just stayed and stayed. An easier option is to just accept that they are at your house and are eating your food. Give up the internal resistance and internal conversation. 'If they mention how successful or clever, they are again, I will have to say something'. Next time keep breathing and practise accepting what is happening. Give up imagining how reality could be better. Reality just is and always happens now.

Anxiety is the anticipation of something to come. It's not happening now but you are concerned about it now. It is happening in your imagination.

"Will I have enough superannuation when I retire?"

"What will I do if I run out of money before I die?"

"What if I forget what to say next?"

The vast majority of people fear public speaking more than death. They fear rejection, ridicule or being recognized as charlatans. It is normal to fear public speaking. It is also normal to fear death. It is entering the unknown. Public speaking can be enjoyable and can benefit others. You have a choice. You have some control. You can decide whether to speak or not. You can also decide which thoughts to engage. Maybe you can't decide which thoughts enter your mind. Once they arrive, you can decide which ones to replay, engage or ignore.

If you are concerned that the audience will judge you, they will whether you speak or not. The person sitting beside you could be judging you. I am sure everyone judges. Again, this is normal behaviour. What people think of you is really not your business. You have no control over what people think of you so accept that being judged by others is a part of life.

It is natural and very common for people to judge each other. It is also natural to be concerned about what people think of you.

Change what you can and accept what you can't. This is easy to say but hard to do. Not impossible. Just hard.

You won't be able to stop people judging you, negatively or positively.

Be careful about getting excited about compliments. The person is still judging you.

Imagine this. You are asked to fill in for a speaker from your organization who has agreed to speak at a meeting of a professional association. The meeting is in two days.

Important people will be present including your CEO. You feel a sinking sensation in the pit of your stomach. You know you must agree for your career's sake but can't help thinking ahead to what might happen if you make a fool of yourself. You know your stuff but hate speaking in front of an audience like this one.

"What if my mind goes blank?" Ahhhh. What if….what if….

You know you won't sleep properly if at all. You wonder how you will find the time to prepare your presentation. Your manager's comment of 'just wing it' isn't helping. Anxiety rules. None of this is really happening but your body is reacting as if it is.

The real problem is not that you have been asked to fill in for a speaker. Your ruminating is the problem. You are fusing with a thought. It is time to defuse and let go.

Cows ruminate. They seem to endlessly chew something in their mouths. We are like cows when we turn over thoughts endlessly.

Fear is a little different from anxiety although similar. Fear is a response to danger or perceived danger. It is natural to be fearful of spiders, large animals, confined spaces, snakes and fire. Include being criticised by others. You can fill in your own list. The fear comes when you encounter the object or situation. Actually, it's your thoughts about the situation that cause the fear. Anxiety is created by your imagination. You get fearful in advance. It happens to everyone. It can be a useful warning providing you don't keep repeating the warning to yourself. Imagine wondering if you remembered to bring your presentation with you as you are driving to the venue or boarding the 'plane "Have you left the lights on?""Did you turn off the heater?"

There are two kinds of fear. Seems there are two kinds of everything.

One is the fear of something bad than can actually harm you. Fear of having an accident, fear of being bitten by a snake, fear of drowning, fear of being injured or dying. This fear is hardwired in your brain to keep you alive. You should have some fear about being harmed. Being fearless would be unwise. Only action heroes are truly fearless because they can't die. You should be frightened of crocodiles, electricity and driving in the rain at night. Take care around these three. Maybe I forgot some. I did forget an important one. It's when your partner or manager says "We need to speak about something important."

Fear is normal and helpful.

The second kind of fear is the one that lives in your imagination and your thoughts. These thoughts can't harm you but will generate the same fear as crocodiles and electricity. You are really frightened by the thought rather than anything real. If a leaf lands on your head in the garden and you think it is a bird eating spider, you will be frightened. If a bird eating spider lands on your head and you think it is a leaf, you won't be frightened. The thought is the problem here or rather the way you are treating the thought. You are giving it credibility. You have activated a primitive response, somewhat unnecessarily. Some people activate the anxiety response so often that it remains switched on all the time. Just tap them on the shoulder and they jump. Ever ready.

I remember speaking to a person I was working with in far north Queensland and told him I had gone for a run along the beach. He said "Be careful. There are crocs on the beach." I had run that morning on the beach he mentioned as dangerous. I had enjoyed the run along a deserted beach. I wasn't scared because I didn't know the risk. I wasn't brave or fearless. I was ignorant. I was cautious the second time I ran along the beach and saw several logs that looked like crocs. I didn't enjoy the run so much the second time and ran faster.

Imagine that you are in a lift and the doors close. The lift doesn't move. For some people this is terrifying because they jump ahead to spending days trapped in a lift. Others wait patiently for the lift to move. If it doesn't, they wait patiently until the lift is fixed. Some people remain calm. Some are disturbed by anxious thoughts and feelings.

"What if the lift fell thirty floors with you inside?" Just jump before it hits the bottom. I know this is an urban myth but so is a lift going into free fall. It can't but this won't stop people having scary thoughts.

I sometimes show people a photo of a very large tarantula. I ask them what they are looking at. People always say "A huge spider". Some even recoil. Actually, it is only a picture of a spider and pictures are harmless. Somehow people have confused a picture with the real thing and get real feelings.

I suspect that spiders are more frightened of us that we are of them. Who's much, much bigger? Despite the difference in size, it is normal to be frightened of spiders. I suspect that the parents of spiders tell them how terrifying humans are.

In which category is the fear of speaking in public?

Is it something that can harm us and cause injury or is it a thought that we can ignore? It is like the picture of the spider. If it can harm us, we should be very careful of public speaking or avoid it altogether. If it is only a thought then we need to accept it as only a thought and simply enjoy the opportunity to be in front of an audience. Mmm…do we control our thoughts? I can't control mine. They seem to come uninvited.

I don't know about you but I don't seem to have much control over the thoughts that come into my mind, awake or asleep. I recently read that the average person has around seventy thousand thoughts each day. How do people measure this? I think I have one thought all day that morphs into thousands. Like spilt mercury.

What I do know about my thoughts is that I can engage them or let them pass. I have no idea of where they are coming from. Some of my dreams are very strange but that is another story…. or book.

Another distraction when speaking is our ego. Our ego is a false self. It is an elaborate thought or complex set of thoughts that want us to believe that if we fail, we will be lesser beings. It wants us to believe that if we speak well, we will become a more important person. If we crash and burn, then we will be failures and drop further down the food chain or management structure. I suspect that our ego is mostly an unhelpful thought. Some ego is fine. Having a realistic opinion about your ability is helpful. Too much and you are out of touch. Making a mistake one time does not make you a mistake and one successful action does not make you a success.

Ego will encourage you to move from failing on one occasion to becoming a failure. Verb to noun.

If you can reflect on the concept of ego then you are not in the grip of your ego. The real you is looking at the false you, the figment. Your ego works unconsciously and is very worried about being seen as important and successful. If you remember that you are really a messenger and not the message, your ego will evaporate as will the fear of failure. If the worst that can happen is not getting your message across this time, there is little to fear and a lot to learn. Figure out what you need to do next time to get your message across and move on. No recriminations. No blame. You missed this time. Accept what happens and learn. You will be successful next time or the time after.

Your ego hates the present. It likes to dwell on past success or failure as a way of building its importance or lack thereof. It also likes to project into the future. Either way, it is avoiding the present. When speaking, the present is your friend. If you focus on what is happening in the present, there is no past or future to worry you or give you a false sense of your importance.

If thoughts pop into your mind just before you stand up to speak, that you could fail like last time or that your manager in the audience will judge you harshly which might lead to your career being stalled or ruined... remember they are only thoughts. These fantasies can't exist in the present. If you are truly focused on what you are doing in the present, thoughts about the past or future won't distract you.

I once spoke at a conference and was sent the feedback from the audience a week later. They filled in a form which was on their seats. There were about one hundred people present. Except for one comment the feedback was positive. One person wrote 'Did not hit the mark'. For a few moments I got stuck with this comment as if it had stuck to my head and I couldn't get rid of it. I could have tried to distract myself. I could have told myself that it was the view of only one person.

I breathed in. Paused for six seconds and then breathed out. The thought went away and only came back when I wrote this.

Let me suggest some exercises to help you control your nerves and maybe even enjoy speaking in public. Believe me, enjoyment is possible.

1. Practise staying in the present during the day. Focus on what is happening not

what has happened or what might happen. If you get negative thoughts, step back and observe that you are having negative thoughts. If you notice what is happening then your ego is not in control. Let the thoughts drift away. Don't fight with them or try to push them away. Let them float away. Let them come and go. Say to yourself "I am having the thought that I ...." When eating a meal, really notice what you are doing. Savour. Don't read while you are eating. Just eat slowly.

2. Find a way of relaxing before a presentation. Really listen to relaxing music. Don't think about the music. Just listen. Submerge yourself in the music. If thoughts distract you, go back to listening to the music.

3. Prepare the first minutes of your presentation very well so that you know that it will flow easily. Maybe start with the purpose of your presentation and rehearse this many times so that it flows easily.

4. Focus on your breathing as you are about to start speaking. Breathe in deeply, pause and then breathe out slowly. The out breath is very important. Count when breathing out from 1 to 5.
5. If you have unhelpful thoughts about public speaking, say to your mind "Thanks for the thought." Maybe you have an unpleasant memory that keeps coming back. Learn from it and let it go. Saying thanks acknowledges that it is a thought and that it is not coming from you. The deeper you.
6. If you insist on looking back and forward, look back with satisfaction. "I have done my best." You can also look forward optimistically. "I am getting better each time I speak." Get back to the present as quickly as you can.
7. Look at fear in all aspects of your life. Has fear of failure held you back from attempting anything that you really wanted to do? In the past, I certainly have let it hold me back

8. So, let's summarise ways of managing fear. Let negative thoughts drift by without engaging them. Give them space. Say to yourself "Here's the thought about…..." Prepare the opening so well you could do it without thinking. Focus on the present. "This is going well." Just relax into your presentation and let the thoughts and words come. Pause to create space for more thoughts to enter your mind. Let your message flow out of you. Breathe out and count from 1 to 5 before you say your opening words. Become a student of mindfulness. Think less. Be more aware. Let unhelpful thoughts pass by without engagement. You won't lose your ability to think if you do it less. On the contrary. The quality of your thinking is likely to improve. It's very difficult to be fully aware of what is happening in the present as well as engage passing thoughts. Your awareness becomes divided if you attempt both. If you are waiting to speak, just observe the audience. If unhelpful thoughts arise, acknowledge them as thoughts. "There's

that thought again" and go back to observing.

You don't want to get rid of thoughts or feelings. You just want to know which ones to engage and which ones to let pass by. If you are like me, you have a steady stream throughout the day and night. They are called dreams at night. Pick out the best ones and focus on them. Let the others drift by.

If you are not able to identify the thoughts that are hindering your performance then the thoughts may have probably become feelings. Identify the feeling that you are calling fear and treat it as you would a thought. Speak to the feeling." Thanks, feeling, for the warning. I appreciate your help

Locate the feeling. Exactly where is it? My feeling is usually in my stomach behind my belly button. We are old friends. For some people, the feeling is in the chest, throat or shoulders. Some people get sweaty hands. Some need another visit to the toilet.

If you get a feeling, where is it exactly? What shape is it?

If you have a recurring thought, or feeling, give it a name. "Ah…here's Otto again." Mine used to be "I'm not good at maths." This thought visited so often that I came to believe it …. for a while.

I know I said I would list some excellent books on Mindfulness and will but couldn't resist mentioning some now.

Mindfulness for Life by Dr Stephen McKenzie and Dr Craig Hassed.

Mindfulness – a practical guide to finding peace in a frantic world" by Mark Williams and Danny Penman.

The Happiness Trap by Dr. Russ Harris

Mindfulness – 23 ways to live in the moment through art by Christophe Andre

Mindfulness – Be mindful. Live in the moment by Gill Hasson

Do you remember the pilot who landed in the Hudson River? His name Is Chesley Sullenberger. The movie is called 'Sully.' You will remember that his aeroplane got into serious trouble after a bird strike. Both engines shut down. He focused on landing his aeroplane and protecting his passengers...and nothing else. He did a great job of landing in the river. He judged that he would not be able to land back at the airport. All 155 passengers and crew survived. He had learned to focus on the job in hand without letting useless thoughts distract him. Admittedly, he had 40 years and 20,000 flying hours experience behind him. He later said "It was very quiet as we worked, my co-pilot and I. We were a team but to have zero thrust coming out of those engines was shocking – the silence."

His friends described him as shy and reticent. Did he feel nothing during the crisis? The mayor of New York City called him Captain Cool.

Reality was different. In a 60 Minutes interview he admitted the moments before the crash were "The worse sickening, pit of your stomach, falling through the floor feeling" that he had ever experienced. He also admitted to suffering symptoms of post-traumatic stress disorder for weeks after the crash, including sleeplessness and flashbacks.

Back to his actions. As US Airways Flight 1549 was sinking slowly, Sullenberger walked the flooding part of the passenger compartment twice to make sure everyone had evacuated before retrieving the maintenance log book. He made sure he was last to leave the aircraft.

Not like the captain of the Costa Concordia.

Somehow Sully had acted calmly despite having almost overwhelming feelings of fear and panic. My guess was that he acknowledged the thoughts and feelings and did not let them take over. He was mindful of what needed to be done to save his passengers and crew.

A few weeks after the crash it was revealed that Sullenberger had left a library book in his luggage. He rang the library to say that the water damaged book had been recovered. They waived the late fees.

He became an international speaker on airline safety. He could easily have become a speaker on mindfulness or not letting unhelpful thoughts and feelings distracting you from the job in hand.

He is passionate about airline safety.

If you choose a topic that you are passionate about it is less likely that you will have to deal with fear. Maybe you will still have to handle unhelpful thoughts and feelings. Choose something that you really know about. I have found that I have fewer fearful thoughts when I stick to what I know and what I am passionate about but this may not be the case for you.

Also trust yourself to get into the zone by speaking from your heart. If you hear distracting voices in your own head like "What are you doing speaking to this group? They know more than you?" Treat the thought like a dog barking in the next backyard or a crying baby on an aeroplane. Just keep doing what you are doing. Just keep speaking. You don't have to think about words or what you are saying when you are in the zone. The message just comes out. Trust yourself.

Have you found that the words come more easily when you are speaking from your heart?

Try dealing with something that annoys you in the same way. Notice it but don't fully engage. "Interesting that I react when this person interrupts." Interesting but not annoying. Maybe you hear the thought "They shouldn't interrupt others." Deciding what others should do or not do is a thought. Accepting what is actually happening will allow you to focus on your task.

Make your task of working with fear a project for the next week. Think of a situation or person that causes you to feel fear or irritation.

Dwell on the situation or person until you get a tingle of fear. Immediately disengage from the thought. Let it go. Say to yourself "There's that thought again". "There's Otto". Be aware of the thought but only aware. If you give a recurring thought a name, you're admitting to yourself that this is a thought that is visiting. "Here's Otto again. Keep breathing when he visits. You decide on how you react to the thought. Breathe out when the feeling starts. It may start in any part of your body.

If public speaking causes fear for you, imagine yourself in front of an audience. Notice the thoughts that arise in your mind. Let them keep moving out of your mind without disturbing them by contradicting them or asking them to go away. They are just like the many thousands that are generated each day and night. For some reason, we generate many, many thoughts, some helpful, some unhelpful, some weird. It's normal.

Sometimes we have entertained unhelpful thoughts and feelings so often that that they appear almost instantly. They can catch us unawares like a car horn when we dose at the lights.

I understand that our minds can process data at a speed of 110 bits per second. A conversation requires around 60 bits per second. We can listen to two conversations at once with some effort but not three. The conclusion here is that if you focus entirely on what you are doing and engage the whole 110 bits, you won't have the computing power to worry or be concerned about yourself. A formula one driver uses all 110 bits. A soccer goal keeper at the highest level uses all 110 bits when defending against a penalty kick. There isn't enough time to wait until the ball is kicked before moving left or right. If you focus all your energy on speaking as well as you can, nothing else exists. You won't be able to reflect until you have finished. Being 100% present and focused has a lot going for it when speaking to an audience.

Try listening to two conversations at once. Careful you don't offend the person nearest to you.

Can you listen to both?

Does the quality of your listening decline?

Can you listen to someone on the telephone while checking your email?

Do you drive at your best while speaking on the telephone?

If you give 100% of your attention to one activity, Zen like focus will slow down your mind and sometimes stops the flow of thoughts altogether. In these moments, you cease to exist in your own mind.

I remember this happening to me in a flotation tank. I was floating in warm water in a completely dark chamber. I found the first period difficult but then seemed to float in my mind as well in my body. The thoughts slowed down and then seemed to stop altogether. I was in the tank for over an hour and it felt like minutes.

We are all blessed with wandering minds. This is normal. Just keep coming back to the task in hand.

How and whether you react to these thoughts is something over which you have some control. Be kind to yourself. Experiment.

Choose wisely.

Here's an exercise for you.

Think of a situation that causes mild concern.

Imagine it is happening right now. Get into the detail. Imagine it visually. Hear the sounds. Hear what people are saying.

Keep breathing. Focus on whether you are breathing in or out.

Go back to the situation.

Go back to your breathing.

Focus on the out breath and count from 5 to 1.

Think of a negative experience in your past and let it drift by. If it sucks you in, pause, breath in deeply and let it pass. Keep practising until it loses its venom. It's like looking at a gorilla at the zoo or a large spider behind a perspex screen. They can't hurt you. Only connecting with the thoughts can distract or hurt you.

I recently asked a person who I was coaching to get ready for something negative I was going to say about them. We were working on using mindfulness to handle negative thoughts. The person immediately held their breath and braced as if I was going to hit them. I didn't say anything negative. The person had anticipated what I was going to say. " You were going to say that you didn't like my………." The person had jumped ahead and engaged with very unhelpful thoughts. Of course, it is natural to brace yourself if you think that criticism is coming your way. Instead of bracing, you could try focusing on your breathing.

Fear is not worthy motivation for avoiding speaking. It isn't even a reason. It is an uncomfortable or painful emotion to warn us of danger. It works better with spiders than public speaking. Imagine getting those two confused. Keep your fear of spiders or at least a healthy respect until you can recognise the poisonous ones or the ones that bite.

Did you know that mosquitoes are more dangerous than sharks?

Millions of people die each year from mosquito bites. A very small number of people die from shark bites yet we are more fearful of sharks than mozzies. The thought of a shark bite seems to be the problem. The thought.

Your parents probably told you that "Sticks and stones will break your bones but names will never hurt you." Names can hurt if you let them.

I remember being told as a child that bullies are actually frightened. It made them easier to deal with. I almost felt sorry for them. They didn't need to be frightened of me. Your audiences could be frightened of you. If you want to test this just ask "Can I have a volunteer to join me on stage?"

So, let's put fear in its place. It is a warning and only a warning. You can make it bigger by focusing on it. You can acknowledge it and let it pass. You can do everything you want and feel the fear that sometimes comes. The risk of feeling fear does not need to be a reason for not doing something you really want to do.

Acknowledge the fear "There's that feeling again."

Feel the fear but don't give it centre stage.

Focus on what you are doing.

Our body give us lots of warnings through the day.

They are only warnings.

3. The Opening. 'Getting off to a good start'

Good morning. I am going to show you how to get off to a good start in your presentations.

It is very important to create an early good impression. Your audience will make a quick decision about whether to listen or not in just a few seconds.

This chapter is called 'Getting off to a good start'.

What I will cover is a simple acronym to help you design your opening as well as ways of acting calmly.

My objective is that you will be able to design an opening that has real impact and encourages your audience to listen to you and take action.

So, there's my opening structure.

What do you think of this opening? I will explain the structure later in the chapter. Let's leave it as an acronym for the moment. INTRO.

Introduction of topic and self

Need – why my information meets your need

Title – I am calling my presentation……

Range – What I will cover today

Objective – By the time I finish, you will be able to….

Imagine that you begin to introduce yourself from your notes and discover that the first page is missing. Panic takes over and you tell the audience that you have lost the first page. Worse still, the previous speaker has taken the notes you left on the lectern. Panic again. "My notes have disappeared!"

Not a good start.

On the other extreme, imagine you are about to start, you look up and the audience is beaming at you even before you open your mouth. Somehow you have won their hearts already. You start and your words come easily and smoothly without any conscious thought. You are in the zone. Your audience is receptive and warm and you are off to a wonderful start.

Take your pick.

You have very little time to connect with your audience. If you connect, they will listen attentively and support you. If you don't, they will turn off or become distracted. They will allow themselves to become derailed by a freight train of thoughts, maybe about your inability to get their interest. More likely they will be absent minded. They will leave mentally. Maybe start texting. There is so much that your audience could be doing rather than listen to you. There is serious competition.

I understand that humans now have the same attention span as goldfish.

Online communication has become an acceptable activity in an audience. People may not answer their telephones but find it OK to go online while you are speaking. You may think they are taking notes about your presentation. Good luck. You can discourage this activity by having a compelling opening. At least give the internet and social media some serious competition.

Your opening is very important and needs to be planned carefully and delivered skilfully.

Do you remember an excellent opening? What exactly did the person do to engage you so quickly? Maybe you don't remember what they did because you were engaged. Perhaps you remember the bad openings because you had time to be critical since there was nothing else to do.

I remember a very unusual opening.

It was a large audience.

The speaker was introduced but seemed distracted with his copious notes. He walked clumsily to the podium but suddenly tripped at the top step. His thick glasses fell on the steps. His notes fell in a heap near the lectern. He got down on his knees and picked up the notes. The audience was stunned. Cathedral like silence.

He nervously shuffled his notes and apologetically started.

"In summary….no, I'm sorry that is the last page!"

It was shaping to be a titanic disaster.

Suddenly, he took off his glasses and announced in a very confident voice "Gotcha didn't I. That is NOT how to start a presentation."

There was enormous relief in the audience. We were frightened that he would continue on as a nervous wreck. He did the opposite and started again. He rescued us from his other self. The opening was so bad it was good.

Let me suggest several openings. You can experiment with all of them and see which ones work for you. A wide range of options is essential for professional speaking as your audiences and their moods will vary.

First up, you need to make sure you are calm. Acting calmly is often spoken about but seldom achieved. I must admit I have rarely felt completely calm when speaking. In the early days I felt anxious. Once I overcame this anxiety, I began to feel excited hoping that the person introducing me would let me get started. I can now feel calm just before starting and it is a good way to feel leading up to a presentation. So, aim for calm. Maybe calm with a dash of excited or calm and assertive.

Your audience will pick up on your mood or emotional state, especially at the start. Your mood is contagious. Make sure it is worth catching. Treat a speaking opportunity as you would any other important event. Get a good night's rest. Make sure you are well prepared. Visit the venue where you will be speaking. Prepare the room to suit yourself. Arrive early. Meet some of your audience beforehand. Stay in the moment. The future will look after itself if you deal with the present. If you are meeting people, focus on the people you are meeting. Hold their gaze as you meet them.

Your audience will catch your mood.

All these activities can become part of your preparation ritual. They are part of mine.

Some things I have tried in the past and work for me include:

1. Listening to music that will help you focus and stay calm.
2. Letting go of negative thoughts and holding on to positive ones.
3. Creating positive thoughts 'I know my topic and this presentation will go well'.

4. Writing and reading your own affirmations 'My message is important. They want to hear what I have to say today'.
5. Telling yourself it is not about you. It's about your message.
6. Keeping your ego out of the situation by focusing on the audience and their needs.
7. Staying in the present. Coming back if you drift into the past or future. Focusing on what is happening around you.
8. Focusing on your breathing.
9. Sitting in a quiet place and being mindful of your surroundings.
10. Breaking your presentation into stages and focusing on each stage e.g. checking the equipment.

Don't jump ahead in your mind.

Some of these work some of the time. I am sure you have heard of them and maybe tried them yourself. Try again. Try new ways of preparing. Create your own ritual.

Do you remember Steve Waugh's red hanky? Do you remember Steve Waugh? In case you don't, he was a very gifted Australian cricketer.

He was a swash-buckling batsman. He had a lucky red handkerchief. Sometimes it poked out of his pocket. It helped him feel confident. Putting it in his pocket was part of his preparation ritual.

I polish my shoes the night before a presentation and create a checklist for the next day's performance. I tick everything off to make sure nothing is forgotten. Extra batteries…tick. Remote for projector…tick. Spare remote…tick. You get the point. Just like going overseas. Passport…TICK. This is my pre mortem.

Do you have a ritual that helps you to reach calm?

Does it work for you?

Anxiety can be a common consequence of agreeing to put yourself in front of an audience. Kidding yourself that you are not anxious will make it worse. Accept how you are feeling and take action to prepare.

In this book, I have shown you ways of handling anxiety based on mindfulness.

Learn to recognise when thoughts are intruding on your calmness.

Identify these as thoughts. Label them. Here is the thought "This audience will judge me harshly." Tell the thought that you know it is a thought. No more. Maybe say "Thanks for the warning."

Let the thought pass by as if it was a passing cloud. Don't engage it. You can look at a snarling dog without touching it. You know not to touch a box jellyfish. You leave a snake in the grass alone. You could avoid conflict by not responding to a critical remark. Let the motorist behind you keep tooting without holding your breath. He wants to turn left and you don't. Same technique. Just focus on your breathing.

Some years ago my wife and I were returning home from an evening with friends. It was 11pm. We were travelling on a major freeway. Suddenly a small car came up behind us travelling at high speed. Admittedly, we were in the right lane as we had just entered the freeway. I pulled over into the centre lane. The small car pulled in front of us and slowed down with the hazard lights blazing. I slowed down too. The car then began to swerve in front of us crossing three lanes. I took a deep breath and decided to slow down further to create more distance between us. The driver continued to swerve for a few more minutes and then took off at high speed. My heart did beat a little faster during the incident. I kept breathing slowly and let a lot of unhelpful thoughts pass through my mind. It was over before it started and I could continue on my way home. Hopefully, no one else encountered the driver on their way home.

What I did was breathe slowly to keep myself from over reacting. I also focused on my driving and let sudden thoughts and feelings pass me like other cars. I held back on judging what sort of person was driving the other car.

Try practising this yourself until this becomes second nature.

Skip the panic step if something goes wrong. Let's say that you are told at the last minute that your CEO will be present. Breathe. Let these thoughts drift by…. or rush by.

'Oh %$#&. I didn't want him there.'

'I am stressed enough already.'

'He/She won't be happy with what I say.'

'I will make a fool of myself.'

'The driver of the other car is an idiot and I wish I had a blue light on the roof of my car.'

Rather than make the effort of fighting these thoughts or replacing them with opposites e.g. 'I am delighted my CEO is in the audience'. Let them float by.

Let the thoughts move along the stream passing through your mind. Watch them as if they were luggage on a carousel at the airport. When you see your suitcase or identify a helpful thought, grab it. Let the others keep moving past you.

Now for some openings.

A common opening for skilled presenters is to use the acronym - INTRO.

I have heard many variations of this acronym.

I used this plan for an opening at the start of this chapter.

Introduction of self and topic. "My name is Paddy Spruce and I am going to speak about." I left out my name at the start of this chapter.

Need. Why this topic is important to you is…. The benefit of knowing this.

Title. I am calling this presentation 'Persuasive Presentations'.

Range. What I am going to cover is…

Objective. By the end of my presentation, you will be able to design and deliver a persuasive presentation.

You can also make friends by assuring them that you will finish on time or a little early.

Be brave. Tell them what they will be able to do at the end of your presentation. Focus on what they will be able to DO.

If you get this INTRO into your memory and begin with it, you will have told your audience everything that they need to know so you can get started.

You will also feel confident because the words are flowing easily.

An unusual opening and one that has significant impact is to start with a story. No mention of who you are or your topic. Jump straight into the story. The story needs to have a link with your topic and focus. Tell the story and then segue into your topic.

For example, I saw a presentation where a safety officer started his story like this:

"Today is the 21st February, 2018, it is a fine, bright day. At exactly 10.05am, there is a hair-raising scream from the back of the factory where the guillotine is situated…."

This was a toolbox talk and the opening grabbed everybody's attention.

Tell your own stories. Make sure you add details and use the present tense. There IS a loud scream gets your attention better than there WAS a loud scream. A hair-raising scream is better than just a scream.

I have also used the technique of beginning with a story and stopping the narrative suddenly to move to the topic, leaving the story incomplete. Story interruptus. The audience will be curious about why you didn't finish the story. What happened?

Towards the end of your presentation, you link back… "You must be wondering what happened to the guillotine operator? Well, an ambulance was called immediately and he did lose a finger but fortunately he is back at work. He is now much more safety conscious and a wiser man."

Practise telling stories with detail to generate interest and make sure there is a point to your story. The purpose of the story is to connect with your audience and prepare them for your presentation and your focal point. You will seldom make more than one point, so make sure you know what the point is. Something like 'quality matters' or 'safety first' or 'treat our customers like guests in your own home' or the customer is not always right'. We want commitment from our staff not compliance.'

A third way of opening is to ask a question.

What is the most dangerous animal in Australia? What is the most dangerous insect?

People will guess…. incorrectly.

Did you know that worldwide, sharks only accounted for 9 deaths in 2020? Seven of these were in Australia. Death by mosquito is over one million each year according to the WHO.

People are terrified of sharks and find mosquitoes annoying. It should be the reverse.

And by the way, humans accounted for 475,000 deaths in 2019. These are the ones we know about.

You can then make the point that people seldom know the facts. You can then segue into presenting some facts about safety, sales or productivity. Ask the question and then present the facts.

A variation of this technique is to present a fact to start. Did you know that the most dangerous insect in Australia is? The bee. We seem to have knocked the mosquito off first place in this country.

Start with a question like "Did you know that we average twenty meetings a month on this floor and the average length of these meetings is two hours? I hope these meetings are productive because they are costing us a lot of money. In fact …"

A final opening technique is to start with a universal statement. A universal statement is one that everyone will agree to. "I am sure we would like to see this organization thrive in these hard times, wouldn't we? We have had a hard year. We have lost some very good staff in the past months. We need to improve our sales performance this year."

These statements seem obvious because they are. The purpose is to get the audience agreeing with you at the start. You might practise with even more obvious statements like… "Here we are at the end of another week. Like every other week, there have been some good and bad results."

Listen to football commentators. They are masters of the obvious. "One team has to win today. Whoever is ahead at the final siren is the winner."

Remember the opening is the opportunity for your audience to decide whether they keep listening or start day dreaming. You do this every time you read an article in the paper or watch the start of a movie. You say to yourself "This looks good" or "I am not going to read this article" or "I will try another channel."

It takes discipline to focus on anything for an extended period. It also takes careful planning and creative thinking to make it easy for an audience to stay engaged. Anyone can get attention for seconds. How to keep their attention is the challenge. Start well and you are half way home. An audience can take seconds to decide whether to get on your bus or wait for the next one. Use these seconds wisely.

Make your opening, memorable, captivating, interesting and unusual. Get started well and everything falls into place.

How do you usually open your presentations?

Does this work?

What have you seen others do that works?

What are you going to try next time as an opening?

What question could you open with?

Do you have a story that you could interrupt at a critical moment and complete at the end?

How could you use this story to make your point?

What could you do to recover from a poor start?

Next time you start a book, movie, video or article…. Notice whether you are engaged. Identify what has happened to engage you. Try to identify what caused this to happen. If you are engaged, you won't be able to identify what got your attention without losing your connection. It should be easier to identify what caused you to disconnect. It may be a comment by the speaker. I immediately disconnect in the evenings when a caller says "This is not a sales call."

Which newspaper articles do you read in full? Do you decide after the first paragraph?

This could also happen at the start of a conversation. Identify exactly what causes you to tune out. Is it something they said or did? Is it a facial expression?

Make sure that everything you say and do has the intention of engaging your audience. You may find that they would respond better to a question rather than listen to your monologue. They may prefer to talk rather than listen.

Create the opportunity for them. Start with a question and wait patiently for the answer.

I once saw a speaker start a presentation with a grounding exercise. She asked people to sit quietly and clear their minds while breathing slowly and deliberately. She wanted us to become more present and focused so that we could listen to her.

It worked a treat for me. She got my undivided attention

Get started on getting started. Start well and you are half way to a successful presentation.

How are you going to start your next presentation?

Are you willing to experiment and move away from your usual openings?

What can you say or do to get immediate interest and full attention?

Look for great openings – books, articles, movies, interviews?

If you find something that works, experiment with it yourself.

4. The Body – 'the message', the content.

Imagine you asked an audience member after your presentation "What did you learn from my presentation?" and they said "Nothing really. I already knew everything you said about the topic. I was hoping to get some new information or ideas but didn't. However, I did like your sense of humour and your colourful slides."

The middle was missing for them. No new content.

Imagine a friend saying to you "Thank you for the present. I just loved the wrapping."

If you start well and finish well, you now need a middle. You need new content or a different way of looking at old content. The middle is the real message. It is the information. It is the evidence that supports your message. It helps to lead your audience to your irrefutable conclusion. It needs to be chunked into bite sized, digestible pieces.

When asked for your mobile number, you automatically chunk the numbers. I tell mine in three chunks. It doesn't sound right in one long stream. When I leave messages on people's answering machines, I very deliberately chunk my number into three bits. This gives them an opportunity to write down the numbers in between. I wish they would do the same for me. I sometimes need to replay a message several times to get the number.

Stew instead of sushi. Stew is all mashed together. You can't have a piece of stew. It is not chunked. Sushi is in very discrete pieces. You can have one piece now and another later with a gap in between.

A simple way of structuring your message is to brainstorm all the information that you could present on your topic. Just get everything down on paper. Stick it notes work well for this activity. You will probably have far too much information but just keep writing. Strangely, some of your best ideas will come late in this process. Nothing is irrelevant at this early stage.

Perhaps sleep after this brainstorm. Insight often comes after deliberate thinking. Your mind will keep thinking when you are asleep. The inventor of the sewing machine saw the hole in the needle in his sleep. Actually, he saw a person holding a spear with a hole in the tip of the spear. Your brain will work when you are asleep, unfettered.

Once you have exhausted all your ideas, identify the sub points or categories. For example, you might divide into past, present and future. You might divide into problems and solutions, advantages and disadvantages, progress over several years or comparison between solutions.

Now reduce your sub points into key words. For example, then – now – tomorrow. I remember an acronym for fear. False Education Appearing Real. You could do a mini speech on each word.

The next step is to break the sub points into mini speeches. These mini speeches have a logical order but could be spaced between a question and answer session. So, three mini speeches with three Q & A sessions, one after each segment. "Now, are there any questions about what I have said so far?"

For example, you could start with the history of the company and then seek questions about the history, then move to the company's present activities followed by questions again and finish with the company's plans for the future with more time for questions.

If you do ask for questions, it is very important that you do get a question. Ask the question and wait…and wait. If all else fails, ask a question yourself. "While you are thinking about a question, I have one for you…."

This is a last resort.

Each mini speech is also broken up into three segments using ERR as an acronym.

E – Explain. Explain the point you are making. For example, 'We need to think differently in today's market'. Explain why we need to think differently to keep our customers happy at a time when people are looking to spend less.

R - Reinforce. Reinforce your point with an example. If you want to make the point that organizations are spending less on R&D or marketing or training, quote an actual example. If you want to make the point that this cutting back is not productive in the longer term you might mention what it would cost to replace skilled workers when the market improves…if they can be found! Think of an example of an organization that has thought differently and thrived in tough times.

R - Recommend. Each mini speech needs to end with a call to action or a close. "So, let's all think of ways of thinking differently to the way we thought last year." "I would like you all to give me an example of how your thinking has changed by tomorrow. I want concrete examples of how you are going to serve our customers differently. We all know that the thinking and activity that got us here will keep us here."

Apply ERR to each of the mini speeches. In a twenty-minute presentation, you will typically include three mini speeches with a Q&A between each mini speech to make sure the audience is with you.

It is risky to leave all your questions to the end of your presentation. They have got used to listening to you rather than participating or answering questions.

Think of a topic that you present on and break it down into three chunks then break these chunks into ERR. Make sure that the call to action at the end leads to the common theme of the three chunks which is the purpose of your presentation. If anything, that you present does not contribute to the purpose of the presentation – scrap it.

You now have the body of your presentation. All that is missing is a captivating opening and a close that will have your audience on their feet clapping.

A good way of improving your chunking is to listen to how other speakers chunk their content. Try putting your next presentation into bite sized pieces…. now. It makes digestion so much easier for your audience.

Chunking is essential for memory. Do you ever have trouble identifying your own telephone number when someone chunks it differently to the way you do? It will sound foreign if not chunked the way you are familiar with. Imagine if someone left a message with their telephone number without pausing in between some of the numbers. You won't be able to remember more than seven or eight numbers unless they are chunked cleverly.

Would you rather hear – 9419187645 or 9419 187 645? Can you remember how to spell

Csikszentmihalyi? He is one of my favourite writers and the author of an excellent book titled 'Flow'. His name means Michael from Saint Csik. Saint Csik is a place. Mihalyi is Michael in Hungarian. This is a hard name to spell but you have some chance if you chunk it.

Csik szent mihalyi

Although the country doesn't exist anymore, I learned to spell Czechoslovakia by chunking. I put Oslo in the middle.

Czech Oslo Vakia

I now want to show you how to structure your presentation in more detail.

There are many ways of structuring. It's the same for books, movies, plays and stories. Whatever structure you use, it needs to have a flow. Left to right. One to ten. Yesterday to tomorrow.

A very obvious structure is to follow the face of a clock. Start with 12 noon and move around clockwise. Prezi can be used instead of PowerPoint or keynote. Finish at midnight. Prezi is ideal for a clock like structure. You can zoom in and out when you want to mention detail. Zooming out is the transition as you move to the next segment or point.

Create a visual that looks like a clock face and follow the perimeter. The three points can be located at 3pm, 6pm and 9pm. Easy to follow and very logical and familiar.

Another familiar structure is a pyramid or triangle. Three points for three points. Perhaps a central theme in the middle. The Karpman Triangle is famous. Persecutor. Victim. Rescuer. Well maybe The Holy Trinity.

An organic structure is to copy the root system of a tree. The roots subdivide and come together as a whole trunk. Start with the roots and end up with the trunk. The trunk is the focus. The roots or branches are the chunks leading to the focus or theme. Growing is a great metaphor. Autumn or Fall can be a down time. Pruning can be cost cutting. Spring is coming as the market picks up. Looks like seasons are another structure.

'Now is the winter of our discontent!'

Another structure is a simple map. Just like a treasure map. Start at the bottom and cross rivers, mountains and forests. Pass through towns and cities to get to your final destination, solution or the gold.

A very obvious structure is problem – solution. Present the problem. Drill into the problem. Break the problem into parts. This will make people aware of the implications of not dealing with the problem and allowing it to get worse. "If we don't fix the problem now, it is likely to happen again." Imagine a technical problem that will affect production or the company's reputation. Imagine leaving a rude person in customer service to do further damage.

When you feel that you have really exposed the problem and all its implications, offer a solution and an implementation plan. Don't offer the solution until you have plumbed the depths of the problem. Uncover the implications. The solution will relieve the tension. The greater the tension, the greater the relief afterwards.

"If we keep allowing spillage into the local creek…."

"Luckily no one was hurt this time. Next time we may not be so lucky. Imagine what it will cost if someone is seriously injured. We must act to make sure this never happens."

A final structure is a story. Narrative is a very important and effective way of structuring a presentation. People like stories in preference to a data dump. A data dump leads to ego and is often caused by ego. By ego I mean Eyes Glazed Over.

It is important to create tension during the story. Something goes wrong. There is a potential crisis. "What can we do now?" The situation gets worse. Hold back on the solution as long as you can. Release the tension with a solution or a happy ending. I have heard so many stories about customer service, health and safety, security, continuous improvement, team morale and inspiration. Organisations hire motivational speakers when they already have their own motivational stories. They just need their own people to step up to the microphone.

A really clever way of telling a story is to jump in and out of the story. I call this Story Interruptus. I mentioned this earlier. Here's what I mean.

Begin the story and continue until you come to the first crisis. Segue out of the story to present some evidence. Imagine you are speaking about calling an ambulance when someone has a suspected stroke. You start your story with a person coming to you for help. Their speech is slurred and they feel strange. Their face looks lopsided. You now segue into your FAST speech.

Face, Arms, Speech, Tongue.

The first thing you notice is that one side of the person's face has dropped. F for Face. This is a symptom of a stroke. Time to call 000. No time to lose.

You then segue back into your story. The person is frightened. You tell them to sit down in your office and keep breathing. You know there is no time to spare. You ask them to lift up both arms. One arm won't co-operate.

A for Arm. One arm is out straight. The other won't obey properly. Time to call 000. No time to lose.

Back to the story. You ask them to tell you when they noticed something was wrong. You can't understand their speech. Their words are slurred. They speak a foreign language but you know they are not multi lingual. Is this the gift of tongues or a stroke?

S for Speech. Slurred speech means it is time to call 000.

You also think to ask them to poke out their tongue. It's doesn't come out straight. It bends to one side. They are becoming more concerned. So are you.

T for Tongue. Call 000.

Of course, you wouldn't work your way through all four as time is of the essence. One is enough.

You would finish with a summary of the four indicators for a stroke and close the story with what happened to the person afterwards. Did they recover fully? Are they back at work? Do they have some continuing speech problems when they are tired? Fortunately, very prompt calling of 000 ensured that the long-term effects were minimal. Delay is dangerous or deadly.

Finish with a call to action.

If you have any suspicion that the person has suffered a stroke, call 000 immediately. Better to be safe than sorry. Immediate action will help with eventual rehabilitation. Delay causes further damage or….

The purpose of this presentation is to save lives and preserve the quality of lives.

ACT IMMEDIATELY.

A presentation like this done properly can save lives. You could save a life.

PowerPoint and keynote offer many structures. Find one that suits your purpose or invent your own.

Now for linking your chunks.

For the clock…. now let's move down to 6pm at the bottom of our clock.

For the triangle…let's drop down to the right-hand point.

For the tree…let's follow this root to the surface.

For the map…let's get back on the bus and drive to the next town.

For problem/solution … let's explore this problem further.

For story telling...so now we knew we were in real trouble. What next? I looked frantically for my mobile to call 000.

PowerPoint, Keynote and Prezi have clever transitions. Your verbal transitions will do the same job. You are saying that we have finished with this segment and it is time for questions or time to move to the next segment or point. People's attention is sharpened and they prepare for another piece of information instead or a continuous, long chunk.

Sushi instead of soup.

Your exercise for this chapter is to chunk your presentation. Three chunks are ideal. Three building blocks. You can prepare your audience for the chunking by saying something like "I am going to show you three ways of reducing the time spent on emails."

Also decide on your transitions. How will you move to the next point, town, number or message? Maybe even move yourself during this transition. Stand in a slightly different place for the second chunk. Make it very clear that you are doing a transition.

Don't be seduced into trying many PowerPoint transitions. They can become annoying. Use a simple transition and stick to the same one for your entire presentation.

Your verbal transitions will work best. If you have been speaking about the past, try something like this…

"NOW LET'S DISCUSS WHAT IS HAPPENING TO OUR COMPANY AT THE MOMENT." Increase the volume to get their attention. Time to get ready for the next exciting segment.

I have known speakers to segment their points with pictures. For example, a picture of a cup of coffee at the coffee break. Or maybe a picture of a bridge or the clock moving to the next number or the tree growing.

Or a yellow brick road!

Do you remember how Dorothy kept meeting strange people on her journey? They each had a problem. One was missing a heart. Another was missing courage. A final one was missing a brain. The dog linked everyone. It was the sensible one who was in touch with reality. What a great story with wide appeal. Everyone got what they needed. Great transitions along the Yellow Brick Road.

There's no place like home.

I told the story of the Wizard of Oz at a graduation once, actually twice. I told them that they were already intelligent before they graduated but that they now had a diploma as evidence. I told them they were born smart and that doubting themselves would hold them back in further pursuits. I jumped between Dorothy's story and their own.

Now is the time to decide on your structure and chunks.

What is the best structure for your presentation?

What are your chunks?

Which transitions will you use? How will you move from point to point?

Will you encourage questions and if so, when?

How will you link your opening with your close?

Can you use a clever acronym for your chunks?

5. The Close. The finale. Pulling it all together.

Have you ever been to a movie and found the ending less than satisfactory? Maybe you felt disappointed or incomplete. You would have preferred a solid close with a call to action or at least a take away message. You really wanted everything to be tidy and locked up with a flash back to let you know the end was really the end.

The curtain didn't come down properly.

I remember a movie where people started murmuring when the credits came up…prematurely. The person beside me said aloud "That can't be the end!" We felt let down. We suspected a sequel. Remember 'The Sixth Sense.'. Sixth Sense is hard to say and it was an even harder to figure out when he died.

I have seen limp closes at conferences. Have you?

"I think I have covered everything. Let me think…. Did I mention…? Um?' Sorry I went over time."

The ending is arguably the most important part of your presentation. The vital ingredients are a quick summary, a call to action and a final message or reminder of the focus of the presentation. Your audience need to know what to do with the information you have given them. If the close is done really well, a person could turn up for the ending and get most of the message. They will have missed the detail, the reinforcing stories, the supporting facts…but they will still get the essence of the message. A good way of approaching the close is to assume that some people have missed everything that has gone before either because they arrived very late or lost interest and went on a mental wander.

You have an opportunity at the end to help people move from what they now know to what they need to do with the information to get results or improvements. Knowing without doing is not going to change anything.

Knowing and doing are often a long way apart. Most people know how to maintain or achieve wellbeing. They know about exercise, mindfulness, meditation, healthy eating, moderate alcohol consumption and enough sleep. Maybe not Mindfulness…yet. They know the risk of speeding. They know but do they do? Knowing without doing can be a waste of good memory. You could do an exam on the topic but don't actually use the information. Imagine how you would react if your new dentist had bad teeth or your financial advisor wanted to borrow money from you to pay for lunch.

Your entire presentation is meant to change behaviour. Maybe changing thinking first and then changing behaviour. You hope that their knowing will lead to doing a few times until a habit is formed. What you say at the end is meant to encourage them to take action and change their habits. This is difficult to do so you need to include a strong, convincing call to action. You want them to turn right instead of left like they usually do. You want then to pause and not do what has been natural to them in the past. Stop smoking, eat better, exercise, do one task at a time, focus on what they are doing, think more optimistically, stop complaining, work as a team, reduce accidents, improve quality, be grateful, let unhelpful thoughts drift by without engagement, delight customers.

A researcher called Ebbinghaus discovered that people's attention wanes in the middle of a presentation or speech. They listen carefully at the opening. They also listen carefully at the close…. if they know when it is coming. If they don't know the end is near, they may still be absent minded as you finish speaking. Imagine missing the final part of a mystery thriller because you fell asleep on an aeroplane. At least they tell you when a plane is about to land even if it is the early hours of the morning. You don't want to be woken by a thump on the runway or a clapping audience.

You need to tell your audience to pay full attention as you are about to summarise and come to a grand conclusion. A simple way of doing this is to lead with something like, "Now let's summarise what I have said so far." "How do we make this happen back at work?" "What do you have to do tomorrow to make sure this happens?" It also helps if you raise your voice at the ending to telegraph that the end is coming. Some may be wondering how to use the information that you have given them so the ending is critical as this is when their thirst is quenched. Relevance rules. You give them something for their headache. You offer a solution. You ask for their commitment to make sure that they take action.

You will need to arouse them at the end to make sure that they know that the most important part is about to happen. I suggest that you prepare the ending first so that your entire presentation is focused on the climax.

Here are the ingredients of a good close.

1. Telegraph that you are about to enter the closing phase.
2. RAISE your voice and your energy.
3. Summarise what you have presented quickly and succinctly.
4. Deliver a strong 'call to action'. "What you need to do today is…"
5. Finish with a story/demonstration/graphic that encapsulates the focus of your message. Make sure that this is an optimistic story or captivating picture that locks in your message in a memorable way.
6. Do whatever you can to get the audience to applaud. If they applaud it means that you have raised their energy at the critical time. It's not about your ego. It's about raising their energy levels at the end.

Remember that the ending is the entire presentation in miniature. You want an individual to say "I am sorry I missed everything except your ending but still got a good sense of your message and focus. Where can I get the details that I missed?"

Next time you present or speak, make the ending the feature. Pull something out of your hat. Maybe they were going to score you a seven but in the last seconds got excited and gave you a ten. People are influenced by critical moments not the entire presentation. This critical moment might be a story, a picture, a demonstration or a mistake. Make your significant moment, the ending, the climax, the finale. How much of your time at secondary school do you remember? You probably remember particular incidents or teachers. Maybe the graduation or mess up day.

People don't remember an entire presentation. They choose critical moments that they remember. They remember events that triggered emotion.

If you don't stir people to action, your presentation will simply be about passing on information with no change likely. No point really.

Imagine a men's football team attending a presentation about respecting women in an effort to reduce domestic violence. Or asking them to intervene when they hear other players speaking disrespectfully about women.

They attend. They get information that they already know about. They get a certificate of attendance. Nothing changes. Time and opportunity are wasted. They have the same lack of respect afterwards. Domestic violence continues.

What a tragedy when the opposite could have happened. They could have been challenged to view all women as their sisters, mothers or wives. They could have been challenged to show their courage by asking their peers to show more respect in their language. Courage on the field is admired. How about some off the field?

I mentioned attending a driving course for advanced driving. The morning was entirely about theory. We saw a video and heard about how to handle a car in a skid. Some people were very active in the discussions and asked a lot of questions. We spent the afternoon on a racing track actually driving cars and practising what we had learned in the classroom. You won't be surprised that some of the silent people did well and some of the talkative people didn't do so well. If you had been the presenter you might have been mistaken if you took the classroom response as an indicator of who was getting the message and could translate it into behaviour behind the wheel. Sometimes introverts rule.

In most presentations the last few seconds matter a lot.

Imagine you are in a job interview and they say at the end. " Do you have any further questions for us?"

Imagine suggesting a new process to your manager. "The last comment I want to make is…"

Imagine ending a sale. "Can I help you with anything else today?"

Finally imagine bringing your presentation to a strong close. "You must be wondering what to do with this information…"

"I don't think I finished my story about the hair-raising scream coming from the back of the factory. Well…"

This way of linking the start of the presentation with the climax helps the audience to recall and remember everything you have said in between. 'Story Interruptus' will stick in their long-term memory. They may have heard the same information many, many times. You tell it in a way that shocks, excites or saddens and action is more likely. Tagging your message with emotion helps recall. Create some emotion and then deliver your important point. The two become entwined forever and make it much easier to recall. Walking past your old primary school will bring on a flood of memories.

Think of people you like or dislike. Former partners. Regrets. High points. Holidays.

"I had heard this many times before but this time seemed different. I decided to take action immediately."

Don't just tell them again.

Tell them differently.

Think of a movie, book, play or game that had a dramatic ending. If you remember it, it had an impact on you.

What was it about the ending that got you in?

Do you remember taking action after hearing something that you had heard before?

I remember hearing a talk about using your brain in a more balanced way. I am right-handed. I wondered what I could teach my left hand to do. The speaker simply asked what we could do to balance ourselves more. They had already convinced us that it was advisable to use our whole brain. Out of the blue, I decided to use my computer mouse with my left hand. This meant that I could write while using the mouse at the same time. I am not sure why this challenge seemed important to me.

It felt very strange and clumsy using my left hand on the mouse. I persevered for about a month until it felt normal. I still use the mouse with my left hand and even draw with my left hand now. I am learning the alphabet backwards, listening to CDs on speaking tourist French, Italian and Spanish in my car instead of listening to the news. I am also writing a book, this one. All this came from a challenge to experiment with new behaviour. All this came from a challenging speaker with a final call to action.

Try new behaviours. Stretch your brain.

You never know when your call to action will hit the mark, shift the entrenched attitude, improve the workplace, improve the world. Maybe I went too far with 'improve the world'. Perhaps just improve your world.

The highlight of my career as a professional speaker has been the occasions when I have heard from people that they took action that improved their situation.

My favourite story which I recall when I have had a difficult day is a true story about a blind high school student who heard me present. He spoke to me later about what career he should pursue. He had heard me finish my talk with something about identifying and following his passion. He had been told that his prospects were limited which they probably were at the time, many years ago.

I asked him what he would do if he were sighted. He answered immediately. "I would want to be a social worker." I challenged him. "So, what's stopping you?" It seemed that some thoughts were getting in the way.

Did I mention that his parents were with him and that he lived in a small country town? Both parents gave me a look of disapproval. I suspect they thought that I was leading him to disappointment and a fall in morale. How could a blind, country boy become a social worker? I asked the three of them to explore the possibilities. I wondered if I had done the right thing for him.

If I had my time over, the only thing I would have done differently would have been to encourage him and his parents to relate to their negative thoughts differently. Instead of trying to change the thoughts as an optimist would, I would have suggested that he recognise the thoughts as merely thoughts and let them pass by. Perhaps even acknowledge them "Thanks Otto for the warning about how hard this is going to be for me. I appreciate your concern. Let me know if you have any other concerns."

This would have given him more energy to do what he did without the worry. This would probably have helped him by calming his parents down.

He had enough on his hands without having to deal with concerned parents.

Many years later, I read an article in the newspaper saying that he had graduated as a social worker and that he was working for an organisation that helped people with disabilities to enter the workforce. The article said that it had been very hard for him as it was early days for blind people to study at University. He was a true pioneer and blazed a path for others in his situation.

I challenged him and his parents without knowing that I was doing so.

He took decisive action that led him to a sighted university environment and years of hard work. I am sure he continues to help and challenge others.

Always ask for ACTION.

So, let's work on your ending.

What are you going to say in your quick summary?

What do you want them to do after you finish?

How will they use the information you have given them?

What story can you tell to bring your presentation to a satisfying conclusion?

What are your final words?

If they forget most of what you say, what do you want them to remember for the rest of their lives? Tell them. "If you remember nothing else from what I have said today……I want you to remember…."

What is your final CALL TO ACTION? Be brave.

Don't leave it to professional speakers to do all the speaking. You know your workplace better than they do. Step up. Speak up.

Develop a signature ending to your presentation.

Do it now. Soon is too far away.

6. Memorable Information. "Making it easy to remember"

Some speakers make it easy to remember what they have said. Some make it easy to forget.

Think about the high and low points in your life. What do you remember? Why do you remember what you remember?

With good presentations, you remember the structure and the content. You know they made three points and gave examples. You remember the focus. You learned an important lesson that will help you for the rest of your life. They challenged you to take action.

About two years ago, I heard a person speak about getting rid of crap in the office. She got our attention. She said crap. She then explained what she meant. Crap was an acronym for **C**ynicism, **R**esentment, **A**pathy and **P**essimism. I remember the structure and the content as if it was yesterday.

Some speakers make it impossible to remember what they have said. In fact, you may not even remember hearing them speak. They expect you to see them while blowing smoke in your face.

Some can put you to sleep. No apparent structure and a lot of words presented in a monotone. This is stream of consciousness speaking. 'Let's see what comes out on the day. I don't need to prepare. I'll wing it.'

The old idea that repetition will aid memory has some truth in it but can become very boring. Don't you hate the repeat television advertisements? Exact repetition creates boredom or resentment. Then again, you do remember them. The question is 'Do you take action?'

If you choose to use repetition, do it with imagination and variation.

OK, so what does a speaker do to make their message memorable?

Keep it Simple (KIS)

Make it Unexpected

Provide Concrete examples

Tell Stories

Keep it Simple.

E=MC2. Maybe you don't know what this equation means but most people remember it because it is simple. How do you remember that a dromedary camel has one hump? It is like a D on its side. The bactrian camel has two humps, like a B on its side. Simple but memorable. If you want people to remember your message, make it very simple.

Once you have decided on your topic, focus and purpose, you need to make it simple. Simple structure. Simple language.

Some people seem to want to sound complicated. Maybe they think we will think they are smart. I don't. I doubt whether they understand what they are saying themselves if they can't speak simply.

I recently heard a speaker use the word 'zeitgeist'. It is a great word but not popular. I think we were supposed to be impressed by the person's vocabulary and multilingual ability. Maybe it was the perfect word to use on this occasion. That is if everyone understood the meaning of the word.

It means 'spirit of the times'.

The three stages of simple are –

Simplistic – too simple. You don't understand so you over simplify. You are doing a book review and pretending that you know more than you do. Some speakers resort to metaphor to explain something they don't understand themselves. 'Your brain is like a computer'.

Complicated – confusing for them. Maybe you fear that people will think you are not very smart unless you sound very smart by using complicated language, slides, information. "You may not make sense of this slide. It's hard to explain (to simple people like you)."

Simple – just right. You know what you are speaking about and are willing to be seen as simple because you are. You really are an expert and have your ego under control. People who really know their stuff speak simply.

Don't you love experts who explain complicated ideas simply and memorably. Gravity, pressure, economics, ethics. Ten commandments into one.

I saw a video clip of a cannon ball and a feather being dropped from a height. Of course, the ball won. The experiment was then done in a vacuum. Now in theory we all know it should be a dead heat but I have always had my doubts. Amazingly, the feather and cannon ball fell together and landed at exactly the same time. Amazing, memorable imagery rather than forgettable theory.

A simple title or structure also helps to get people in the right frame of mind.

'Ten simple ways to save on your energy bills.'

Keep going down the road to simple until you are simple yourself. Don't take yourself seriously.

Good humour is simple. Nothing too clever unless you doubt your own intelligence and want to sound smart.

Is your message simple? Is the title simple? If not, how can you make it simple?

Which movie are you more likely to attend?

'The incredible lightness of being'

'Black Hawk Down'

'The Magnificent Seven'

'Lion'

Maybe 'Snakes on a 'plane' is too simple.

Go over your presentation and simplify everything.

'How to' titles are popular.

'How to lose 10kg in one week.'

'How to double your superannuation in a decade.'

'How to reduce your water bill by half.'

These all sound simple, don't they?

Presenters who really understand their topic can risk being simple. Simple is good.

People who don't understand their topic fully like to sound complicated. They think it makes them sound intelligent. It doesn't.

Have you used simple words and sentences?

Are your ideas simple?

Is your language simple? Reader's Digest simple?

If you are wise you can afford to be simple. Wise means that you understand your topic well enough to show people how to use the information to improve their work performance and their lives.

If you don't know your topic well, you may have to hide behind big words and abstract concepts and hope that no one notices.

Yeah right!

Let's apply this to your presentation.

Is your message simple? Is the title simple? If not, how can you make it simple?

These are simple messages that we all know and hopefully…do.

Slip, slop, slap.

Eat locally grown food

Drink water

Sleep eight hours

Eat real food

Call 000 FAST

Make it Unexpected.

For some reason, people will laugh if led verbally in a direction but suddenly redirected with an unexpected twist.

'My husband would never leave me. He is too loving, too loyal and…too lazy.'

'The vet said she had to put our dog down…because he is so heavy.'

If you deliberately lead people along a thinking path and create an unexpected turn at the end, they will remember. There is shock and surprise value. Your body becomes instantly alert and focuses in a second.

Imagine saying that you and your partner had never had an argument in twenty years ….and then you met.

Think about what you consider unusual. Housing design, colours. news items, dogs that walk on their hind legs, solutions to problems. Street names. Sometimes one country's usual is another's unusual. Would you eat frog's legs? Why do we have chocolate frogs?

You see how easily unusual comes to mind. You can see usual all day and not notice. One unusual sticks.

Imagine trying to sell a car in Spanish speaking countries if the car was called a 'Nova.' Means no go in Spanish. It can also mean new in other languages so beware.

You would remember a town called 1770, wouldn't you? It's in Queensland and it's where Captain Cook landed for his second visit.

It is easy to be usual and copy everyone else.

Make the effort to use unusual whenever you can. Start out predictable and then twist.

Unusual is so easy to remember. Did you have a student at your school who had an unusual name like Dylan or Desiree? These names stick in your memory, don't they?

Don't ask about Pajero. The Nissan Tiida was not a big seller. Qashqai? People can remember the name but it may not lead to sales. Unusual names with horse connections seems to work with cars like Bronco, Mustang, Colt.

German cars like the wind. Golf, Passat, Scirocco. These are winds. Skoda has a car called 'Superb'. Unusual name for a car. Sometimes numbers are easier to remember. Series 1,3, 4, 5, 7.

How can you lead your audience and suddenly change direction unexpectedly?

Would these unusual titles stick in your memory?

'How to waste money when buying a computer'.

'How to put on 10kg in a week'.'

'How to become a pessimist'

'Why goal setting is bad for your health'.

Many years ago, I heard a presentation titled 'Elephants don't bite' from a wonderful speaker called Joel Weldon. His point was that it is not the big things in a presentation that cause grief when they go wrong. You could probably cope with the power going off for a few moments. It is the small things, the mosquitoes, that cause more grief. A word incorrectly spelt.

Don't you worry a little in an Italian restaurant when spaghetti is spelt incorrectly in the menu?

Sharks account for very few deaths worldwide. Mosquitoes account for millions. Watch out for mosquitoes. Forget sharks.

So unusual does make things stick in memory.

You might just attend presentations with unusual titles out of curiosity. You are likely to remember the titles because they are unusual or unexpected.

What is unusual about your presentation or title?

What is unusual about the way you present? What is unusual about the way you look or sound?

How can you make your information different, memorable and unusual?

I remember attending a conference in Florida. Several people stood out. One in particular was dressed as a cowboy. Ten-gallon hat, cowboy boots, midnight cowboy shirt, saddle bags. You could see him amongst many hundreds of people in suits.

He had a 'ranch' that ran courses on financial management.

Unusual sticks out in our memories.

Provide Concrete Examples.

Abstractions like love, processes, facilitation, industry, management and leadership are hard to nail down and therefore hard to remember. What does it mean to say that Industry has an opinion?

It is much easier to remember blood, a hammer, an apple or Roger Federer. Some people can speak in abstractions for lengthy periods. They utilize, facilitate, commentate and abstract their message into oblivion. I have trouble understanding how a computer works so I compare it to simpler, more concrete machine, an abacus. In fact, I find the human brain so hard to figure out that I compare it to a computer with feelings. Try coming up with some concrete examples yourself.

A business is like a…

Our organization is like a…

Our country is like a….

Would you rather draw productivity or a toothbrush?

What about explaining the purpose of government or the fire brigade? You could do the fire brigade in two words. 'Save lives.'

I remember hearing a speaker compare an organization to a human body. He spoke about disease, toxicity, injuries, healing, seeking professional help and a poor immune system. Some of the cures for a sick body are equally relevant to a sick organization.

Next time you present, decide which part you want to make memorable and use a technique to make this particular point very memorable. "If you remember nothing else, I want you to remember this one fact.

If you are brave, you could check a week later to see if people remembered the one fact that you want them to embed in their long-term memory.

I read that the median amount in super in Australia is $110K. This article also said that a retired couple need around $60,000 per annum to maintain a modest lifestyle in retirement. Perfect if you plan for a very short life.

Do you need any more information if you are young and wondering how much to put into your superannuation fund?

You can also use concrete props on stage to make your point. Not props made of concrete but concrete props. I remember one person explaining how helicopters take off and land. I sort of understood until he took a small helicopter from a box and demonstrated. It became crystal clear. It actually flew and did everything he had told us about. It did hit the ceiling, if you are wondering.

I also watched the launch of the new Tesla S. The founder, Elon Musk was explaining how the technology works. He suddenly said "It would be better to show you an actual car." Amazingly, the bottom of the car appeared on stage without the body so the electric motors and batteries were visible. He didn't need to say any more.

Think about memories that have endured for you and identify how they were put into your memory. What helped move them from your short-term memory to long term memory? The process of putting in memories assists in the process of extracting memories. How you put them determines whether or how you get them out. If you apply some emotional glue to your information it will be easier to remember. Emotion is the glue that makes memories sticky.

Become a speaker known for creating sticky memories.

"I heard you speak years ago and still remember what you said".

Next time you present, decide what you want them to remember, accepting that they won't remember everything and make your information and message memorable, sticky and unforgettable. What has stuck in your memory for a lifetime? Why?

Imagine you are a relationship counsellor and a couple ask you to help improve their relationship. Sounds a bit like they can leave the relationship with you and leave together. You call when it is fixed and they can pick it up, unless you have a delivery service. Relationship is not a very concrete word but looks like one, grammatically. It looks like a noun. Computer is more concrete. You can leave a computer that needs fixing and pick it up later.

I remember attending a course where a participant suggested we play BS bingo. She gave us a list of words or phrases like —

Bottom line

Culture

Multitasking

Competency based

Task oriented

Performance outcome

She suggested we keep count of the number of times the speaker used the phrase or word and called out 'bingo' when we got to ten. She assured us that the presenter would enjoy the joke and was a personal friend.

The presenter hadn't gone long before someone called out 'Bingo'.

When presenting, try very hard to use concrete words and take care when introducing abstract concepts. If you must, use concrete examples. Simple and concrete always trumps complicated and abstract. The risk in using simple words is that people may think that you are simple. They will understand. The risk in using complicated, abstract words is that people will not understand. You choose. Big, woolly words don't make you sound smarter. On the contrary.

Some professions have invented their own vocabulary. Some still use Latin. You need to pay them to explain the advice they are giving you. Imagine calling a calf muscle a medial gastrocnemius. Even spell check doesn't recognise this word. Get the point?

So, go over your presentation and play BS bingo with what you have written. Take out the woolly words and concepts. Take out the fog. If the meaning of a word is not immediately obvious, use another word. Most words have a fog index. Dog, cat and possum are ones. We all know what a dog is. Relationship, industry and management are tens. Use ones.

Tell Stories.

Did your parents tell you about the boy who cried wolf? Did they tell you that it wasn't about you? It was.

Fairy tales and stories have a purpose and a message. The Boy Who Cried Wolf story is told in many countries and in many languages.

Sometimes the wolf is another animal depending on which local animal is 'the bad guy'. Maybe in Australia it should be 'The child who cried Red Back spider.' The message is embedded in the story. It is not a frontal attack that you can defend against. The message slips in the back door of your mind.

I remember hearing the story of how Apple went from selling one off computers to students to mass production. When Jobs decided he needed a CEO, he approached John Sculley. Sculley was the vice president of PepsiCo at the time. The story goes that he was asked by Steven Jobs. "Do you want to spend the rest of your working life selling sugared water or do you want a chance to change the world?"

Sculley joined Apple as CEO on April 8th, 1983.

This is a great story and seems largely factual.

People love stories. You can captivate an audience by starting with a story. Jump straight in. Use your own stories. Give the background. Introduce the problem. Solve the problem. Tell them the moral of the story.

The point behind my story is…….

Can you start your presentation with a story?

Can you use a story to reinforce your points?

Can you promote your products or your organisation by repeating what someone said about your products or organisation? "She told me that she has never seen a product like ours anywhere in the world."

You are not saying this. Someone else is.

So, remember to make your presentation memorable.

So, remember to use simple, unusual and concrete and don't forget to weave in your stories.

If a picture is worth a thousand words, a story is worth ten times more.

We can think in concepts but find it hard to recall them accurately. You think you understand but find it difficult to explain to someone else. " I understand but can't explain."

Really?

Give me concrete, simple or unusual any day.

If I had a choice, I would go for story telling every time with a flavour of concrete, simple and unusual.

Don't use other people's stories if your own are better.

They usually are.

Now go over your presentation and simplify it.

Is the title simple and unusual?

Are your main ideas presented simply?

Have you used humour unexpectedly?

Have you included concrete examples of your main points?

Have you used stories to reinforce your main message?

Do you know what your main message is?

When using visuals, do you build the information gradually rather than showing it all at once?

Do you use plain and simple language?

7. Visual Support "The power of pictures"

Have you ever died from PowerPoint? Maybe got a little sick?

We all know the limits of PowerPoint. We also know the power of pictures to support a message. We all have pictures in our minds of significant occasions.

The picture of the young girl running from the War in Vietnam.

The picture of the Chinese protestor in front of the tank in Tiananmen Square.

Man on the moon.

9/11.

These pictures say it all. They replace thousands of words.

Remember that visual support is simply support. It does not take the place of speaking.

You need to decide on your message and then reinforce it with strong visuals.

One third of the human brain is dedicated to vision. What more do you need to know? If your brain has to decide whether to focus on seeing or hearing, you know which one wins every time.

Imagine someone saying 'Yes' with their voice but saying 'No' with their head shake.

Apparently, about 80% of four-year-old children tell lies. You need to watch their face very closely. I am sure you have heard the story about the boy who rang his school to say that his son could not attend school because he was ill. When asked who he was, he said "This is my father calling".

Visuals are very important in presenting your message.

If you plan to create handouts for your audience it may not include pictures. I suggest that you use three documents.

1, A PowerPoint or keynote presentation which is for the audience.

2. A handout with more detail that is left out of the presentation.

3. A road map or prompter for you to remember what to say.

Don't use one document for all three purposes.

I have seen presentations with nothing but photos or pictures. The words come from the speaker. The fewer the words on the screen, the better. None is ideal. People can't listen to the speaker and also read words on the screen. They choose between one or the other. They can't do both at the same time.

Doing both is multitasking which doesn't work if you want people to remember what you are saying. If you show a picture, give your audience time to look at it without interrupting them.

Let me say that again **"It is not possible for the audience to listen to you and read what you are showing on the screen at the same time!"**

They will do one or the other. They can't do both. They may jump between the two and miss bits. You'd better hope they don't miss the important bits.

If you want people to read, stop speaking. Better still, show a picture and deliver your message verbally. The picture is meant to reinforce what you are saying. They can look at a picture and listen to you at the same time.

Al Gore does this well. He shows pictures which reinforce what he is saying. It is possible to look at his pictures and also listen to him. The two become linked in your mind…. forever.

It borders on insulting to put words on the screen and read them to your audience. Don't insult their intelligence. Encourage them to use it. Choose clever pictures as examples of your points.

"Here is an example of what I mean…." is a good lead into showing a picture.

Ideally, you show photos that you have taken yourself. Authenticity trumps professionalism. They go well together. Maybe it's a dead heat for first place.

A novel way of presenting with only pictures is called Pecha Kucha. Have look at www.pecha-kucha.org The formula is twenty pictures for twenty seconds each. Very few or no words. The pictures change automatically. The speaker keeps up with the slides. Six minutes, forty seconds for the entire presentation timed to the second. You could insert a short Pecha Kucha in a longer presentation to add variety. You don't have to stick to the formula. Invent your own. Put in a short version of Pecha Kucha as a way of varying your style.

If you want to see some very professional use of visuals, have a look at the TED presentations. (TED talks) Some TED presenters don't use visuals.

So, remember that the visuals are only there for support. They are not the presentation.

If you have no visuals then you become the visual. You had better be able to display a wide range of emotions with your face and body. Be careful about your default facial expression. It might be grumpy.

Use visuals wisely. They are a wonderful tool but can become a distraction or a crutch if overused.

Words on the screen are not a picture. Reading the words aloud is like a remedial English class. Demeaning. People can read at several hundred words a minute, at least. If you read the words at one hundred words a minute, they have finished reading as you begin. They now have nothing to do except listen to you speaking very slowly and repeating what they just read. They might also decide to text a friend.

I remember an excellent presentation where the speaker used photos that he had taken himself throughout his forty-minute presentation. Not a single word on the screen. He followed the photos and told stories about what we were looking at. "Now here is a photo of me opening the store on Easter Sunday…."

A good picture is worth a lot more than thousands of words.

There are many sources of good pictures available online. Take care to protect the intellectual property of others. You may be infringing copyright by downloading some pictures. Many are available for a nominal fee. Taking your own photos is easiest. Keep a camera with you or use your mobile. People will recognise that this is an authentic photo. They will take delight in recognising familiar people and places.

A good source of pictures and photos is www.istockphotos.com

They also have short video clips on a wide variety of topics which you can include in your visual presentation. Unsplash.com has some wonderful nature pictures.

How can you make your PowerPoint, keynote or Prezi more pictorial and less verbal? Did I mention Prezi as an alternative to PowerPoint and Keynote? Some people love Prezi and some get sea sick as it is quite different.

Can you try Pecha Kucha in your next presentation? A typical Pecha Kucha presentation is snappy, engaging and leaves you wanting to ask questions. You could just include several photos in automatic mode and explain what people are looking at. Pecha Kucha allows you to time your presentation to the second.

Can you use your own photos to make a point? "You can see how dangerous this exposed edge is to a passerby."

Can you start with a picture that shows your main point at a glimpse?

Would a short video clip embedded in your PowerPoint or keynote help bring home your message?

Safety, productivity, service, respect, innovation? Use pictures in place of these words.

You need to decide whether to use positive or negative examples?

It depends whether you want them to copy or avoid. Using both is clever.

"Does this look safe to you?"

"Now you can see how this has been made it much safer."

Examine your presentation closely and identify places where pictures would have much more impact than mere words.

How can you make your salient point have more visual impact?

"Here's what can happen if maintenance is not done regularly."

"Look at the damage done by the fire in just a few minutes."

"Look how tidy this workstation is."

"How could anyone find anything on this desk?"

"Look at the quality of the finish."

The pictures allow you to improvise. They serve as a guide. If you are not sure of which picture to speak about next, just pause and look. You can set up your display to see the next slide or print out your presentation.

Unwise to say " I don't know which picture is next." It could sound like you have never done the presentation before and that it was prepared by someone else.

I am sure you know that you can jump slides by entering the number of the slide you want and pressing enter. If you want the audience to look at you without the distraction of a slide in the background, press B for a black screen or W for a white screen.

An excellent way to improve your use of visuals is to get help from a genuine expert.

Nancy Duarte is a genuine expert.

She has written two wonderful books. Both contain colourful examples of effective imagery that supports an important message. She has advice on creating a new slide ideology and shows how to use diagrams, colour, movement, myths, arrangement of elements and how to interact with your slides.

Her two books are:

Resonate

Slide:ology

The publisher is Wiley.

There have been murmurs over several years that PowerPoint is dead. Even some that it can cause death. You've heard about 'Death by PowerPoint'. I am sure these reports are exaggerated. Maybe some little deaths. If you call 'bored to death' and 'nodding off' as deaths, then the reports are not exaggerated. I suspect that some people who have trouble going to sleep have tried watching the usual business PowerPoint presentation as the solution.

Professor John Sweller from the University of New South Wales said in 2007:

"The use of PowerPoint presentation has been a disaster. It should be ditched."

It hasn't been ditched.

Would you ditch an excellent tool because people were not using it properly? Would you get rid of mobile phones because people are making calls when driving. How about getting rid of laptops because people use social media when at work?

Good tool. Poor usage.

Putting text on a slide and reading it to the audience slowly smacks of disrespect for the audience. It would work if the audience were illiterate. Speed readers can read up to 7000 words per minute. You probably speak at 150 to 300 words a minute. You are asking a greyhound to crawl like a snail.

Reading from the slide is the equivalent of reading your script to the audience. Equally boring.

Research supports the idea that it is very difficult for people to digest information when it is presented verbally and visually…. simultaneously. They choose or jump between the two.

Another genuine expert is Garr Reynolds. He offers suggestions about design, narrative, focus, simplicity, the clever use of slides and visual support to enhance your message.

His book is called:

Presentationzen.

The publisher is New Riders.

You will need to read the book a few times to see the value of his ideas. The pictures alone make this book a valuable resource for any presenter.

One interesting idea on displaying images comes from the 'Golden mean'. This is a design technique that helps add symmetry or asymmetry to your slides. An image in the centre of the slide does not always have the desired impact. You may pay more attention to the background, sides or corners of the sides. Look at some of the best photographs or paintings. Often, the important figure is not central. What I mean is, the important part of the image is not always in the middle. In some famous paintings, something significant is happening in the background.

Also be careful about what is behind you when you are presenting. If the previous speaker left their words on the board behind you, the audience will be tempted to look past you and miss what you are saying. Make sure there are no distractions behind you.

At one stage, I got interested in why some countries eat better and live longer than others. Okinawa featured strongly. The people live a long time because they eat well. It seems that how much they eat is also a factor. They leave the table before they have filled their stomachs. This is called 'Hara hachi bu' in Japanese. It means 'stomach 80% full'. Leave a little room for something more instead of filling up and feeling full. They also eat good food which they grow themselves. I understand that this is changing with the advent of fast food. A pity.

I got this information from Garr Reynold's book 'Presentationzen'.

I wondered how to put this idea on a slide.

A person pushing back from the table with the meal unfinished?

A plate with some food remaining on the plate?

A small meal on a plate, maybe sushi?

Show the words in Japanese 'Hara hachi bu'.

Show a thin Okinawan eating a small meal?

Put up '80%' on a slide.

You want a picture that will raise the audience's interest and curiosity. A picture that you can explain to make your point. You will see some great examples in 'Presentationzen'.

Spend a moment now to think of a picture you could use to make the point that we need to let our appetites guide our eating not the amount of food on our plates. Less is healthier. There is nothing wrong with leaving the table a little hungry. You know what it feels like to eat too much.

I grew up believing that I needed to eat everything that was put on my plate.

Not anymore. 80% full now.

This also applies to presenting information. Make sure you audience leaves the room still wanting more information. 80% full. You want them feeling curious not over filled. You don't want them thinking or saying, "Stop talking. You have made your point…many times."

Rather. "Please keep going. I am very interested in what you have to say." "Can I speak to you during the lunch break?"

So, use more pictures.

Make your own pictures and photos.

Find and use great pictures.

Use pictures to get an audience response. "What do you think is happening here?"

Use cartoons.

Use colour.

Make your use of visuals a signature strength.

If you plan to write on a whiteboard or paper, use a thick pen and learn to write quickly and artistically. Go to a calligraphy course.

Try this now….

Think about your topics for a presentation.

Think about pictures that will support your main point

Replace some of your words with pictures.

Practise speaking with a picture instead of words on the screen

Keep your mobile or camera with you at all times and take pictures that will enhance your presentation.

Prepare a Pecha Kucha presentation. This is an automated presentation with a twenty second delay using pictures only. You will need to keep up with the pictures.

A picture is indeed worth a thousand words. I suspect a lot more than one thousand. 'Words on a screen' looks like you forgot to bring your notes. A good picture or photograph can bring your presentation to life.

A fancy font never becomes a picture.

Some years ago, I began a presentation with a picture of a mining town in Western Australia. I intended to start with a story of an incident that happened in this town. This was my first slide. As I showed the slide, I began my story. The picture reinforced my story and my point. In fact, it reminded me to start with the story.

Try this yourself. Choose a good picture and a good story. You will have the audience's interest immediately.

Include photos that you have taken yourself in your next presentation.

Any ideas?

What about a visual that encapsulates your message?

For the next week, pay particular attention to the visuals that other people use. If they don't use visuals, ask yourself how they could have enhanced their presentation with good visuals.

8. The Famous Five (mistakes) 'Avoid these at all costs'

Have you ever made a mistake that you regretted to this day? When speaking or presenting, have you done something that you don't even like thinking about?

This chapter is about identifying common mistakes and how to avoid them in future.

Maybe there are more than five common mistakes. These are the five I have seen most often in my career of speaking.

No central point

No real benefit to the audience

No logical flow

Way too much detail

Way Too long

They could all fit under the heading of 'too much ego or self-interest'.

Let me spell out what I mean and offer solutions to make sure you don't make these mistakes more than once.

No central point.

Have you ever sat through a speech and had no idea of the central point or purpose of the presentation? Sometimes you thought a point would appear but then it would disappear in a mist of words without meaning or direction. A question to ask yourself when someone is speaking is 'what point is this person making?' A pointless presentation wastes everyone's time.

A good speech has a strong point that is very obvious. A good speaker will make the point several times in different ways. You are never in doubt about the point that is being made. You know what you are meant to take away. You may even know what action you are meant to take after the presentation.

Imagine that you have a speaking coach who will ask you "What is the main point you are going to make during your presentation? " Maybe, "What is the point of your presentation?" If you only make one point during your presentation, what do you want it to be? What is your focus?' Why are you making this presentation? What is your purpose?

Don't open your mouth until you are very clear about the main point and purpose of your presentation.

Be ready for someone to ask you before you begin "What is the most important point that you want to make during your presentation?"

This even helps in a conversation or argument. If you are brave enough, next time you are in a discussion and want to stem the torrent of words coming at you, simply ask "What is your point?" Ask nicely.

I remember a conference where I was the opening speaker. I had forty minutes. Just before I got up to speak, the CEO who was sitting beside me told me he wanted to say a few words. His few words went for ten minutes. There was no point to his speech. He just rambled. I think he liked speaking to his 'troops' whenever he could. He would have had more impact if he prepared more and spoke less and had a central point each time he spoke. He liked to wing it. No one was brave enough to suggest that he clip his wings, including me.

When I get a call in the evening with a lot of background noise I usually ask "What is the purpose of this call?" If they say "This is not a sales call", I hang up. Be honest about your purpose.

No real benefit to the audience.

I recently bought a new mobile. The salesperson was very young and technically competent. Before I had clarified what I wanted, he showed me an expensive smart phone that had many features. You could even fold it in half. I suspect that he was on a commission and would make more commission if I bought a more expensive phone. There was little value in the benefits he mentioned to me as I simply wanted to replace a lost mobile with few of the features he mentioned. He was really selling to himself. He did not mention any features that appealed to me or even try to identify my needs. The benefits obviously appealed to him. Maybe I should have sold him his phone.

As a speaker, it is essential that you understand the needs of your audience and provide them with information that will be beneficial to them. How will your information help them to get what they want or avoid what they don't want?

Will their situation be improved when you finish speaking?

Imagine trying to convince an eighteen-year-old to invest in superannuation or an eighty-year-old to buy a gaming console. They may be interested but you would need luck on your side. You will need to understand their needs and then promote benefits that have meaning for them to take luck out of the equation. At eighteen, they are unlikely to be concerned about how they will support themselves in their retirement. I only said unlikely.

The same for an audience. Everything you say to them will need to be beneficial to them. I remember hearing a very senior CEO from overseas speaking to a large audience about the company's profits worldwide. The audience had just been through a very tough round of negotiations on salary increase and had been told that the company couldn't afford any salary increases. There was no benefit for the audience to listen to a word he said. He was just big noting himself and annoying the audience. His world view did not sit well with their local view.

Ask yourself when preparing your speech or presentation 'What is the benefit to my audience if they listen to me?' How will they be better off when they have finished listening to me? If you're brave, you could start with a statement like "By the end of my presentation, you will know how to save a thousand dollars a year on your energy bills". Or, "By the end of my speech you will know how to halve the time spent on email." Tell the audience the benefit and be brave enough to tell them that they will achieve the benefit by the completion of your talk.

Be brave.

Aren't you impressed when a sportsperson tells you what they are going to do in advance and then does it? Blue ball inside pocket. Knockout in third round. Six from last ball of the over. Penalty kick into top right-hand corner of the net. Three pointer in the last five seconds. Try it yourself and make sure that the benefit is for them and not you.

Be very clear in your mind how the audience will be better off when you finish speaking.

No Logical Flow

Maybe this is the most obvious mistake. The speaker goes straight into the middle of the presentation, stops and then introduces themself as an afterthought. Or maybe they conclude and then restart because something was left out. No clear beginning or satisfying end. It is deeply dissatisfying to have a speaker end abruptly because they have run out of time. Leaving out the summary and conclusion is a hanging offence. Make sure that you have a flowing presentation that leads people to your conclusion and tell them when you have got there. If you have tangents during your presentation, tell people when they are back into the main body. Link everything. Have a clear beginning, middle and end. Think like a barrister presenting a defence. Start at the start and move to a conclusion in a logical fashion.

Have you ever heard a speaker ask an audience to help them remember where they are? I don't mean which geographic location although I have been in an audience when the speaker had to check which city they were in. I mean that they lose their place and ask "Have I already mentioned when we are starting the roll out of the new product?"

If the flow is disrupted, you may lose confidence in the speaker. They need to know what they have said and convince us that there is a logical flow, just like a tour guide. "Today we are visiting three beautiful towns. The first town is ……. We will then stop for coffee and then head off to the second town which is…. where we will have lunch. We will have a toilet stop in between the two towns.." You get the picture. Imagine if the driver said to the people on the tour "Where are we? Have we visited the second town yet? I can't remember if we have seen the penguins yet. I am sorry we can't stop for a toilet break." You'd get off the bus, wouldn't you?

Too much detail.

This is simply showing off how clever you are as a way of reinforcing your ego. Either that or you haven't prepared and tell people everything you know on a topic hoping they will take something away. You are using an axe instead of a scalpel. This is the shotgun technique.

Only present as much detail as necessary to make your point and only as much as your audience will understand. Better too little than too much. Too little and they will seek you out for more detail. Too much and they have turned off or tuned out. The detail is important. Provide just enough to make your point and not a word more. Leave them hungry and wanting more. 80% full.

I am sure you have seen slides with too much detail. Some speakers even apologise for showing too much detail. "I know there is too much detail here but I will try to explain what it means." Yeah right!'

I have even heard "I can't read this word myself." (I didn't prepare this PowerPoint presentation or look at it beforehand to prepare)

I am sure you have seen a complicated graph in several colours without an explanation. Sometimes the print is too small to read even for the speaker. Maybe the colours are too similar to tell the difference. Why bother?

You get lost trying to follow the coloured line when it crosses another coloured line of a similar colour.

Why would anyone do this to an audience?

Lazy

Don't understand the information themselves

Didn't have time to prepare

Trying to impress

Overestimated their ability to explain the information on the day

More interested in showing how clever they are than informing their audience

Just don't understand how to present simply and succinctly

Underestimated the intelligence of their audience.

Some professions seem to have a habit of giving too much detail and using language that needs explaining. You know who I am talking about. I won't say more or I will get into trouble.

Too long.

Do you ever feel like asking a speaker these two questions?

Haven't you got a watch?

Did you time your presentation when you were preparing?

A presentation is too long when the speaker is still speaking and the audience has stopped listening. Find out how much time you have to speak and don't go a second over. You may even need to leave out information to stick to the allocated time. If you agree to a finish time, honour it even if you have to leave out some content. Maybe decide in advance what will be left out if you run out of time.

I remember one speaker who was last at a conference. They had lost some of their time because the previous speaker has gone over time. The speaker knew that people were tired and keen to go home or to the airport. The speaker simply said "I know you are tired and keen to get on your way so I will just present my main points and make the full presentation available online." The audience applauded.

Sometimes the questions will slow you down and you run out of time. If you do intend to allow time for questions, don't do this at the end. Either allow questions along the way or near the end. You need to conclude with a summary and call to action and this should come after the question time if you allow this. Questions will gobble up your time.

If you do allow for questions, be careful that you don't go over time. Some questions from your audience are really statements or speeches. You will need to be firm and keep your answers short. No harm in telling people that you will stick around after the presentations to answer questions (that don't need an audience). I do remember asking a visiting speaker a question in a break. He said in a loud voice "I am answering some questions in case you want to join us." He must have felt that speaking to just one person was not a good use of his time or wisdom.

If you feel pressed for time, don't make apologies. 'I am sorry I have not been given enough time'. Use the time you have asked for or been given. Start on time and finish on time. If you feel strongly that you have not been given enough time, don't accept the job or ask for more time. As an MC, I have seen speakers ignore my time warning and take as much as they needed causing the next speaker to lose time. I recently stood beside a speaker who had gone over time. I kept edging closer to him, hoping he would take the hint. He didn't. I had to mention that we were out of time. Awkward for both of us but necessary.

If your audience has stopped listening. Stop speaking. Imagine that you are the last speaker and the audience is exhausted. They will love you for finishing early. Make your points briefly and say "I see you are tired from a long day; I will be brief and let you go a little early. Is that OK?"

Cover your ears for the deafening YES.

I remember one conference where I was the first speaker and had forty-five minutes. The MC decided to warm up the audience instead of introducing me. They asked what people had done since yesterday, whether they had had a good sleep. Then got them to sit quietly and clear their minds before introducing me.

I lost fifteen minutes. I had timed my presentation closely and now had to make instant changes.

Fortunately, I was able to jump slides. When using PowerPoint or keynote, you punch in the number of the slide and hit enter. For example, jump from slide ten to slide twenty in two key strokes instead of racing through several slides in front of your audience. I mentioned this earlier. Of course, if you plan to do this, you will need to know the number of each slide.

I would have preferred that the MC tell me in advance that they were going to do a warm up session or an early mind clearing meditation or both. That way I could have prepared in advance.

I did understand that the MC wanted the audience ready for a new day.

If you ever work as an MC, remember that you also need to stick to your timing or everyone following you loses time and the day comes to a crunch ending.

Sometimes senior executives are tempted to speak for longer than agreed because they believe that what they say will make a difference. Sometimes they do. Sometimes they don't.

If the speaking smacks of self-promotion or ego, the effect can be counterproductive.

Ego is a false sense of importance. You believe that you know more or are more than your audience. Imagine how important someone thinks they are if they have no point and simply 'wing it', don't think about the benefit to their audience, jump around in the flow of information, dump data without any sifting for relevance and keep talking until they get hungry or thirsty. Not you. Them.

I remember one speaker at a conference telling the audience that he would speak through the morning tea break because his information was critically important. He asked the audience if they minded. I didn't hear a strong positive response from where I sat. There was no verbal response. He kept speaking. No one was brave enough to tell him to stop, including me.

We just complained to each other over a shortened lunch.

At the risk of being negative, for the next week, identify people using the five mistakes and think of what you could do to eliminate these mistakes. For example, to avoid the 'no point' mistake, start off with the statement. "The main point of my presentation is…." " The benefit to you of knowing what I am saying is…." Start with an introduction and then explain the reasons for the change. Only give enough detail to generate interest. They can research the rest themselves.

"I am going to finish a little early today to give you a chance to reflect on what I have presented."

It's not about you. You are only the messenger. The message is what matters.

Next presentation, do this audit first:

1. Is my main point clear to me and them?
2. Do I plan to present my information as a benefit to them?
3. Does my design flow from start to finish? Is it seamless?
4. Have I provided just enough detail to make my point?
5. Have I timed my talk and allowed for questions?
6. Do I want to have questions?

Finally ask yourself 'Why am I doing this presentation?"

If they are not better off when you finish or you do not improve their situation, you have got some work to do before you present again.

Don't bore your audience. This is the presenter's oath.

They must be better off when you finish than when you started or you have wasted their time…and yours.

Use your time wisely.

9. Mindful Listening

What's listening got to do with speaking? Why would a speaker need to be a good listener?

Has an audience member ever disagreed openly with what you are saying? If so, you needed to quickly shift from speaking to listening mode. The audience might be upset by something that happened before you arrived. They may not be in the mood to listen to you. They may already know what you are telling them. They may agree with everything you say. It would help if you knew what was happening in the minds of your audience.

The best speakers I know are also good listeners. There is a vital link. Good listening goes with humility, curiosity, a desire to learn, respect for the opinions of others and an open mind, all strengths for a speaker.

Listening to an audience is a necessary skill for a speaker. An audience can communicate as one. For example, when they laugh. They become united in humour. It is easy to tell if your humour is working. Just listen. Silence means you are not funny.

Same for their enthusiasm, disappointment, disbelief, acceptance and rejection. Even their silence has meaning. Imagine that you ask a question and get silence as a response. They either don't know the answer or don't want to participate. Maybe they are all introverts. If you listen and watch, you will get some idea of which it is.

Have you ever spoken to a hostile audience? Some speakers will notice the vibe. Others will push on oblivious. A good listener can get out of themselves and see and hear the world from another's perspective. They have empathy. You need empathy to connect with an audience.

I remember starting a keynote presentation at 9am and seeing a lone hand raised in the audience. I had only said a few words. The hand was too obvious to ignore so I invited the question. A grumpy voice said "What time do we finish?"

I hope this never happens to you.

Isn't it strange that we learn to speak but not to listen? No one assumes that we can teach ourselves to speak. There does seem to be an assumption that listening comes naturally like crawling.

Listening is critical to learning, building relationships, customer service, selling, receiving feedback, leadership, raising children and speaking to an audience of any size.

Reality is different for everyone. There is no objective reality. We don't see things as they are. We see things as we are. It's the same for listening. We hear things as we are. Sometimes we hear what we want to hear rather than what is being said. At least some of the message is in the tone. Some people seem to be tone deaf. Others are super sensitive. Email is tone deaf. Imagine thinking that the audience liked your presentation and they didn't or vice versa.

Four years ago, my wife bought a car. She did her research online as we do nowadays. She knew about the car. The salesman insisted on telling her everything she already knew. One question would have saved time and the sale. "What do you need to know?" or "How much do you know about the car?" "How can I help you today?" Any question instead of a stream of technical information. His only question ended the sale. "I can do a little better on the trade in providing you are ready to make a decision today. Are you ready to make a decision today?" Nah! Not with you anyway.'

Listening, really listening is hard. It demands an ability to focus and stop the internal dialogue (Do you wonder who is talking when you engage in this conversation with yourself?)

It also demands enough ego to ask the questions but not too much. Too much will make you defensive about your opinions. You will see them as the truth which must be defended.

As a speaker, you are passing on valuable information for the benefit of others. If you want them to listen to you, you need to listen to them at every opportunity. Reciprocate. Model the behaviour you want from them. Sometimes an audience speaks clearly as one. Tune in. Imagine saying something like "Who is earning less than they are worth?'.

Listen to the silence. You might get laughter or a groan.

Another requirement is being curious rather than knowing everything. Don't you struggle to cope with people who know everything? Their hard disk is full. There is nothing for them to learn so there is no point in your speaking to them. You are supposed to listen to their wisdom. Speakers who know everything are difficult to listen to. Those who admit to ignorance are more believable. They know what they know and know what they don't know. They don't know everything. They can learn from an audience. They ask questions… other than rhetorical ones. They seem to appreciate questions even if they don't know the answer. They are genuinely humble.

Mindful listening is the ability to give 100% attention to what is being said without anticipating, looking for loopholes, jumping ahead (I know what you are going to say!). It includes turning off all internal dialogue (He's contradicting himself!). It means being open to whatever is being said through the word, tone, gesture, facial expression and pauses.

This is too much to cope with unconsciously. This is a bit like driving. It is better for you to just let the message flow over you without getting stuck on one mode e.g., the literal words. You might hear two messages. One from the person's head. Another from their heart.

'I do want to start my own business but am scared that I might fail.'

'I love the quality but can't justify the price'.

Imagine someone at work asking you "Do you feel like working back for a few hours tonight?" This isn't a question. Sure, the words and grammar make it look like a question. Believe me, it's a least a request or maybe a demand.

How would you answer a question from an audience like. " Don't take this the wrong way but why do we have to listen to something we already know?"

So, get in listening shape. Be open to questions from the audience. Invite questions from any audience. You will get a sense immediately of whether they are agreeing with or even understanding your message.

Practise being open to any conversation. Listen more than you speak. If thoughts arise like 'I don't agree with what you are saying'. Let the thought go. You are only listening to a person's opinion. It is OK for people to have opinions that are different from yours isn't it? You don't have to correct them or eradicate ignorance unless a voice in your head demands that you correct people on the spot. How can people survive if they don't know the capital of

Albania? I suspect they will even if you don't correct or educate them. Survive, I mean. I don't know the capital of Albania.

OK, some mistakes need correcting immediately. If they are confused about your message from the front of the room and you gauge this from their questions, it is important that you give them the correct information. Apologise for creating the confusion and ask if you can explain again. Follow up with "Have I explained myself better this time?"

You could still practise listening before making the correction. Ask questions first "Do you know what the company policy is on using Facebook during working hours?" "There is no policy." "Are you sure?' or "So you are saying that we don't have a policy?" Now you can correct the person if necessary. You'd be surprised how much you can influence others by simply asking questions. The best speakers and sales people are usually expert at asking the right questions and listening to the answer. Some speakers start their presentations with a question. Sometimes rhetorical, sometimes not.

You can also practise focusing on almost anything to improve your ability to listen mindfully. You could focus on your body. How is your foot feeling? The left one. Are you breathing in or out? This will lock you into the present and keep distracting thoughts from taking root in your awareness. You could also try an external focus. Look at an object without labelling it.... for sixty seconds. You will see more. Try tuning into what you can hear. What else can you hear? Can you hear the tone contradicting the spoken word? Again, let the thoughts drift by. This is good discipline to apply when listening to an individual or an audience.

Undivided attention is awesome.

I remember hearing a story about a speaker who had to use an interpreter when speaking to a large audience. He spoke briefly and then the interpreter spoke to the audience in their own language. He got used to the pauses and the delayed reaction. He became more confident and thought he'd try a funny story. The story took a while so he asked the interpreter to wait until he had finished before doing the translation.

He told the story slowly and it took a while. He then indicated to the interpreter to translate.

The interpreter said only a few words and the audience laughed out loud. He was bemused. The interpreter couldn't have told the story in full.

During the break, the speaker took the interpreter aside and asked him how he had managed to condense his story into a few words, assuming that they somehow still got the humour. The interpreter said "I thought the story was too long so I simply told them that you had told a funny story and could they please laugh".

So there, listening works in any language.

Sometimes a rising inflection at the end of a sentence means the person has not finished speaking. Sometimes it is a habit. A pause will sort out the difference in your mind. I was once asked if I lived in Melbourne A. Actually, the person was asking if I lived in Melbourne eh? I didn't know that Melbourne was divided alphabetically.

If you don't listen because you have a voice in your head, leave ruminating to the ruminants. Just attend and be aware. Don't get ahead of the person who is speaking. Don't pay attention to the voice in your head that says "I know what this person is going to say next." Even if you do. You don't really. You are just guessing. If you really do have ESP, you are truly gifted.

Five minutes a day will make a significant difference. Clear your mind. Even if the person is not speaking to you, you can still practise. Try the people at the next table. You can hear people in your audience speaking to the person sitting beside them. Maybe this is eavesdropping. It is still practice. Practise next time you take a taxi. Amazing what you will learn. Taxi drivers have opinions on everything.

Next time you are asked a question when speaking to a group, try this….

Pause

Take a breath.

Focus 100% - Give your full attention to the person and their question.

Say 'Thank you for the question'

If you really believe it is a good question, say so. If not, don't.

Paraphrase the question to make sure you have understood it.

"'So, you are asking if we have a new model coming out this calendar year? Is that right?"

Answer the question if you can, briefly. This is not an opportunity to launch into a speech. Short question. Short answer.

If you can't answer the question, admit this and offer to provide an answer at a later date. The audience won't chase you for an answer if you are ignorant. They also may say "'You should know the answer." You can agree to this and offer to get an answer for them. It's difficult to argue with someone who is agreeing with you.

Check that your response is OK.

"Have I answered your question?"

"Can I contact you tomorrow with an answer?"

When ignorance is bliss …

Become a student of Mindfulness. It will help you focus and do everything you do with 100% attention. Multi-tasking is absent mindedness at least partially. Equivalent to .08 alcohol in your blood, I'm told.

Become a mindful listener even if you are the speaker. Listen to the response to everything you say. Watch for reactions. Anticipate questions. Watch for people wanting to ask questions. Be brave.

"The person third from the right, you look like you have a question."

Eat when you eat. Read when you read. Drive when you drive.

Listen to silence. Listen to sounds without labelling.

Pause before responding to questions.

Try it now. What can you hear?

Next time you are in front of an audience, listen to them before you start speaking. Trust your intuition. Imagine that you have ESP. Look around. Listen. Sniff.

Try this exercise now.

Sit quietly.

Make sure you are comfortable.

Breathe in and out slowly several times.

Ground your feet and put your hands on your lap.

Focus on the sounds around you.

Leave them as sounds without labelling them.

If you do find yourself thinking 'That is a truck', just go back to focusing on your breathing.

Now back to focusing on the sounds around you…without identifying the source.

Were you able to listen without labelling?

You can't fail at this exercise. If you keep getting distracted or keep labelling, you are actually practising. Failing would be to give up and stand up. If you remain sitting and moving from breathing to listening to labelling and back to breathing, you are practising and succeeding.

Try this for two to three minutes each day. Your ability to focus will improve as will your ability to listen.

Have you ever ruined a sunset moment?

Have you ever been knocked out by the beauty of a sunset and stopped the wow by having a thought like 'I must do this more often?' Or 'I wish ... was with me?' You could simply go back to enjoying next time. Try it with eating or drinking. Just taste without the labels. Listen without judging.

You will have made significant progress when someone says "For a speaker, you are an excellent listener."

10. Script or Impromptu?

Some years ago, I agreed to a speaking engagement on the topic of the difference between men and women. It was a popular and risky topic. Obviously, I couldn't present both perspectives, so I asked my wife, who is also a speaker, to co-present

I have never spoken with her before, on stage I mean, and didn't know how she prepared. She is also a professional, classically trained mezzo soprano. I mention this because her preparation style is similar for speaking and singing.

We decided on our format and prepared the content separately.

Shortly before the event, my wife asked me to clarify when we were going to swap the microphone or change batons. I think I said something like "I will just say, now over to Hilary."

She told me it would be better if I could give her my script so that she knew exactly which words would lead into my transferring over to her. She was surprised when I told her I didn't have a script. I told her I left it to my brain to come up with the exact words.

She has an extraordinary ability to remember her script. I don't. I speak impromptu. I improvise. Her script was well written and delivered word perfect. I worked around my headings and spoke conversationally. I knew what I wanted to say and just let it come out.

Incidentally, Hilary can also improvise.

If I were in a Shakespearean play, Shakespeare would not recognise what I was saying. It would be similar to what he wrote. Similar. Hilary would be word perfect.

Two very different styles. Both have advantages and disadvantages. I have tried using a script but sound wooden if I read it and stumble if I try to remember it.

I remember watching the Oscars. You know the format. Actors come on stage to receive awards. These are professional actors. I thought they could all speak impromptu. They obviously can't.

Some read from a small piece of paper with 'ums'.
Some stumbled and forgot some names they should have mentioned.

One simply said "Thank you" and walked off.
One seemed to be reading something from his lap.

I thought it very strange that they wouldn't have prepared a speech and committed it to memory like a movie or TV script. Maybe they didn't want to look arrogant by assuming that they would win. Admittedly, they did look genuinely surprised. Oh well, they are actors and obviously don't ever work impromptu except for Woody Allen who doesn't go to the awards.

The host at the Oscars, who is a comedian, looked like he was speaking 'off the cuff'. But who knows, maybe he was also scripted and not speaking impromptu at all. It seems that actors are not trusted to speak impromptu unless they are in a movie produced and directed by someone like Woody Allen and have been chosen because they can speak off the cuff.

I feel much freer working without a script.

The preparation style that works for me looks like this …

I dump everything that I might say onto paper. Let's say my topic is 'How to become an excellent listener'. I put down everything that comes to mind. Stick it notes are useful for this purpose.

What is listening?
Why listen?
Why is listening difficult?
How can we stop our attention from wandering?
Which professions are the best listeners?
How do you improve your listening skills?

This continues until I run out of ideas. Sometimes I get more ideas for days afterwards.

I then go back over what I have written and put the information into chunks. Obvious chunks might be – what is listening, why do we need to listen and how do we improve. Three chunks framed as questions.

If you were speaking about your organization, the chunks might be – our history, what we are doing at the moment and what we have planned for the future.

I structure the chunks in a logical format. Past, present, future.

I often use PowerPoint or keynote to help me remember the structure. I will start with a picture of the past and remember to say 'Now let's look at our history – we started in 2005 …'

I now deliver the presentation using the slides and keep going even if I make mistakes. This helps me develop what I am going to say. Not exactly but close to. I do rely on my brain to find the words. It usually does. If I lose the next word, I pause and it comes.

I know what I want to say and just let the words come out. I don't mind if I make small errors in practising my delivery. I treat it as a conversation between the audience and I. I have a structure to follow in my mind or on the screen but can easily make changes on the trot. I have timed my presentation and will check my timing throughout by discretely checking a digital timer or my laptop timer.

In chapter 4 'The Body', I mentioned using an acronym like INTRO to help your memory. The structure might be firm but the actual words you use might be slightly different every time you give the same presentation. This keeps the energy flowing and the delivery fresh.

If I notice that I am using fillers like…
You know
Like
Um
Ah
Bottom line
At the end of the day

I simply pause when I feel a filler coming on. I hear it in my head but it does not come out of my mouth.

I can remember counting fillers in secondary school. We had a maths teacher who couldn't say similarly. He used to say simirarly. We counted and compared scores in the break. I suppose that counting in a math class is not a complete waste of time. I don't want people counting my filler words and comparing scores after my presentation.

If you use fillers to fill the gaps, try pausing when you about to pop in a 'you know' or a 'at the end of the day'. Pausing really does create interest in what is going to follow the pause. Leave the audience wondering if you have lost your place.

I remember hearing a very well-known and older speaker in the USA. I sense that the audience regarded him highly by the applause at the start before he started speaking.

Very early in the presentation he tried to refer to the city he was in. Something like "I am delighted to be here in …" He paused for a long time. Suddenly a voice from the audience called out "Orlando". The speaker said "Thank you". This happened several times and got a laugh each time. To this day, I don't know if the speaker was having memory lapses or whether he was deliberately pausing.

I did the same thing myself in Melbourne. I introduced a famous former footballer who was pausing. This time I believed that his memory was failing so I fed him some details. He thanked me later. The audience probably thought we were a double act.

Maybe it was time for him to use a modified script with names and dates.

So, you need to decide whether you want to speak from a script or impromptu. Both are possible in the same presentation. You could practise when introducing people. I work as an MC and will stick to a prepared script with some speakers if they want me to do this. I will read through this introduction several times so that I can look up during the delivery. I will also speak impromptu if the speaker has not prepared an introduction. I just make sure I can say their name. NG and Nguyen tripped me the first time. I worked overtime on Fuchs.

Occasionally I fall back on favourites like "Sometimes I say that it gives me pleasure to introduce a speaker when it doesn't. On this occasion, it really does give me pleasure because I have heard … speak before and really enjoyed their presentation. Please join me in welcoming … to the microphone."

Once you have done this a few times, it comes out easier. Just keep doing it and it becomes second nature.

If you are asked to MC or introduce a speaker, be brave and see what comes out of your mouth on the day. You will surprise yourself. If you can introduce someone in your imagination you can do it in reality and aloud.

Try scripting and speaking impromptu and see which you prefer. Maybe do both. Read well from a prepared script with energy and emphasis and then move into impromptu when you put down the script. Pick it up again if your brain freezes.

The advantage of speaking impromptu is the spontaneity and sincerity that is obvious. The disadvantage is the risk of losing your way.

The advantage of being scripted is that you know exactly what you are going to say. The disadvantage is the stilted delivery style or the language which may be better suited to writing.

A combination of the two is a good solution. A map to help in case you lose your way and mindfulness techniques to calm your nerves when you put the map aside.

If you can speak impromptu to one person over lunch, you can speak to hundreds with the same ease … unless you let unhelpful thoughts hinder your conversation.

Try this.

Imagine you are going to say something about a friend or partner as a special occasion like an anniversary.

Start speaking aloud now.

"I have been asked to say a few words about … on this special occasion. I first met … some years ago, in a …"

Keep going yourself. Don't worry if you stall or make a mistake. Just keep going. The ideas and words will come. It they don't, just pause until they do.

Remember the movies stars who fumble. People admire them for their genuineness and lack of script.

The more you speak impromptu, the easier it will become.

Trust yourself.

I remember doing this once and starting with "…. has three amazing qualities." The first two were easy but I couldn't think of a third one so I said to the audience "What do you think the third quality is?" I got several suggestions and agreed with them all.

If you do throw the discussion open to the audience, you need to do it with confidence. You don't need to be confident. You just need to appear confident. Be bold.

Have another go before finishing this chapter.

Imagine it is a significant birthday for you and you have been asked to say something to your friends and family. Or imagine you are asked to say a few words about your manager who is leaving. You have been chosen at the last minute.

Say it aloud now. Don't be afraid to pause while you think of what to say next. No one knows what is happening in your head. They might think you are pausing for effect to build up tension.

Be brave.

Remember that if you can speak to one person without a script you can speak to many, without a script. If the audience looks large. Close your eyes for a moment. Singers do it often.

If you are convinced that you cannot speak impromptu, let me try once more to encourage you.

At my wife's birthday, I gave a speech. Her name is Hilary so I used her name as an acronym.

H for Happy
I for Intelligent
L for Loving
A for Always willing to help anyone in need
R for Resolute and determined
Y for Youthful in her thinking

I didn't need notes in my hand.

Try making up your own acronyms.

You will remember my example of a speaker wanting to get rid of CRAP in the office (cynicism, resentment, apathy and pessimism) The audience will get the acronym and look forward to the next letter. They won't mind if you make a mistake.

You may find that the most critical person in the room is you.

Your audience want you to succeed.

Do what they want.

If you help them get what they want, they are very likely to return the favour.

Over the next weeks, gauge whether the people you hear speak in public are scripted or impromptu or a combination of both.

Some will obviously read their notes.

Some will look up from their reading and speak off the cuff.

Some will seem to be speaking completely spontaneously. If you are feeling bold, ask them if they were scripted. Ask how they remembered what to say.

Learn from them.

You know what you want to say. Just let it come out.

Here is a final quick exercise. Imagine you have been asked to say a few words about a friend/partner/ work colleague/manager at their birthday party.

Try it now. Aloud.

11. Trouble shooting

Imagine this ... You are about to start your presentation at a conference. You are being introduced and getting yourself mentally ready to launch your exciting opening phrase. Your PowerPoint is ready to go behind you on a large screen.

Suddenly...all the lights go off except for the small exit lights above the rear exit door. There is stunned silence!

Have you ever had anything go wrong when presenting or preparing for a presentation?

I am not a pessimist. I am a realistic optimist. I used to be an optimist but realism has crept in. Maybe it's age or sage.

I know from experience that things go wrong. I expect everything to go smoothly but am ready if it doesn't.

For example, I always arrive early and take a book with me. If everything goes according to plan, I have some time to read. If things go wrong, I have time to fix the problem.

Three years ago, I was booked to speak at a large conference at Jeff's Shed. The main plenary was at 9am. My first session was at 11am. I turned up at 8am to make sure I got a parking space and to familiarise myself with the room and the equipment. I had given my mobile number to the organiser the day before. It rang at 8.15am.

"Can you get in early and MC the first plenary session as our in-company MC has had an attack of gastro. How long will it take you to get to the venue?"

Imagine their delight when I told them I was already in the main conference theatre sitting up the back talking to the AV technician and would be delighted to MC the first plenary session.

So, let me mention some things that can go wrong and how to deal with them.

The foundation of trouble shooting is calmness. Calm comes from accepting what is happening without making it worse. No fretting. No wasted energy complaining. Stuff happens. Accept it and take action. Fix it.

It also comes from understanding the difference between pressure and stress. Pressure is OK and part of everyday living. A deadline is pressure. It motivates us. An exam is pressure. Limited time to prepare for a presentation is pressure. All doable. If you have been given limited time to prepare, either reject the offer or accept and deal with the pressure.

Stress is pressure plus ruminating. P + R = Stress. Stress is not good.

A deadline with ruminating sounds like 'I am not going to make this deadline'. Limited time to prepare accompanied by 'This presentation is going to be a disaster', is not a helpful way to prepare mentally. You are generating the ruminations so you can ignore them. The deadline is actual. The negative ruminations are created by your mind. Rumination is the ingredient that turns Pressure into Stress. Deadline into deathline.

Imagine being stuck in a lift. Inconvenient. The air con is working. You can speak to someone in the microphone in the lift. They tell you help is on the way and you may be delayed for a while. This actually happened to my wife and I in a maternity hospital. We were close to having a child and the lift jammed. The nurse accompanying us felt faint and told us she had claustrophobia. We couldn't do much except wait for the lift to get fixed. We got to the delivery room with a half hour to spare. Nothing bad was actually happening. It could have got worse but it didn't.

We could have made the situation much worse by thinking about the lift falling to the ground floor or running out of air or becoming dehydrated or having a baby in a lift. I think the nurse was doing some serious ruminating and feeling light headed as a result.

What if your data projector suddenly stops working? What if the remote for your projector dies? What if you are in the wrong room?

Your pulse increases and you think about how bad a situation you are in. 'I am in serious trouble if I can't get this projector to work.' Are you really in serious trouble yet?

Now…can you control these thoughts?

Imagine that you arrive at the venue for your presentation. The building is closed although you did check the day before and were told that the door would be open and reception would direct you to the right room. The door is closed and there is no reception.

You call the person who is your contact.

You are told you are not at the right place.

Now comes the avalanche of unhelpful thoughts.

Who is at fault?

Did I make a mistake?

How will I get to the right venue on time?

I won't have time to prepare or check the equipment?

They will think I am unprofessional.

Should I cancel?

What excuse will I make?

Should I fake an anxiety attack?

Should I take a taxi and leave my car in the car park?

Is my memory failing?

Early dementia?

Armageddon?

It will take a lot of energy to combat each thought. You don't need an internal debate with yourself when you should be on your bike.

A rational process might look like this ...

Define the problem.

Define your objective.

Consider alternatives.

Choose the best one.

Get started.

I am at the wrong venue

I need to travel to the right venue and I have one hour to get my car out of the car park and start driving using the shortest route.

I need to call my contact and tell them I may be delayed.

I should tell them that I will keep them informed about my arrival time.

That's it. No ruminating or blaming. You can do that later if you really want to (I'm kidding).

Treat these thoughts as uninvited callers to your office. Leave the door to the waiting room open so they can leave if they get bored. Let them come into your office if they are helpful. Let them wait if they aren't helpful. Remember they came uninvited. If you were sitting at a park bench and people kept walking past you, you don't need to be distracted if you went to the park to relax. Let them pass with minimal or zero attention.

If you hear people mumbling near your workstation, just breathe. Notice whether you are breathing in or out. Each time you hear them, focus on your breathing again. Let go on the out breath.

You can practise this any time you are kept waiting. Instead of 'How rude to keep me waiting', say to yourself 'Am I breathing in or out?'

This actually happened to me. Well not exactly this but close.

I was booked to speak at a conference in Malaysia with people flying in from Singapore, Hong Kong, India, Pakistan and Indonesia.

I am normally well organised and also believe in using experts to do what they do best.

I was flying into Kuala Lumpur a day before my conference.

I gave my ticket and passport to the woman at the airport reception at Melbourne airport.

She pushed it back to me. She said in a very matter of fact tone "You can't fly with that passport today. You don't have six months grace." I checked the date and she was right. I had five months. One month short.

I had left it to my travel agent and had not double checked myself.

It was my responsibility to verify everything and I hadn't.

I went through my decision-making process very quickly. I accepted that I would not be flying internationally for a week. I must admit that I had a flashing thought that the person behind the desk would say "Don't worry about your passport this time. Make sure this doesn't happen again."

I called the organiser in KL who was not amused.

To cut a long story short, I flew a week later and presented to an audience who seemed unaffected at the inconvenience.

I learnt a lot from the experience and am more careful now. I must seem pessimistic to some people. I really did learn to manage my thoughts better. This was character building stuff.

On another occasion, my flight was delayed from Melbourne and I was in a taxi in Sydney at the time the presentation should have started at Darling Harbour. I kept the conference organiser informed as I got closer to the venue. I did arrive late but the audience had been given a task that related to my presentation. They seemed OK. Stuff happens. The conference organiser was pleased that I had kept them informed. I had suggested coming up the day before but they felt that was unnecessary.

So, what can go wrong and what can you do to fix the problem?

In every situation, stay calm and use the decision-making process. Manage your ruminations. Let the unhelpful thoughts wither through lack of attention.

Let's look more closely at what can go wrong and what you can do to prevent or recover gracefully.

1. Technology failure.

This covers a multitude of problems. It may include computers, projectors, microphones, remote devices, lighting, heating, lifts, blinds etc.

Often Murphy's law applies. Sometimes I think that Murphy was an optimist or at least, a realist.

Learn to use your own equipment. Know its foibles. Have a backup plan. Two computers, two projectors, two remotes, extra batteries, your own microphone. Make sure everything works as soon as you arrive. For a smaller audience. maybe take your own sound system just in case.

Send a copy of your presentation on ahead and have a backup copy on a USB as well as the one on your computer.

Introduce yourself to the technician. Most conference venues will have a technician on hand. Find out if they plan to stay in the room or wander. Find out where they wander to during the day. Make sure they don't arrive after you start your presentation. They often dress in black so you might not see them leave the room in the dark. Find out their name so you can ask them personally for help during your presentation. Four years ago I spoke at a conference and was told by the technician that the remote would be on the lectern. I was following another speaker with no time in between to check. The remote wasn't on the lectern so I could simply say "Hi Michael, where exactly ..."

If you are presenting on someone's premises, make sure there is someone who can help in case of technology failure. Someone who knows how the equipment works. Ask that this person be present when you arrive and be available during your presentation. If you are there all day, ask for their mobile number.

Be extra careful that your version of PowerPoint is the same as the one on the computer in the room. Better still, take your own computer. If you use a Mac, you already know the occasional problem with incompatibility and will bring your own computer. Some technicians are still Mac phobic but this is changing. When asked, I send my presentation to the client in PowerPoint format and take my own computer with the presentation in PowerPoint and keynote formats. Take your own connections.

Maybe you now think I am overdoing it. Better to be safe than sorry.

Once I spoke at a conference and shortly after starting a warning came up on the screen for all to see to say the battery was about to die. For some reason, the conference organiser had not connected the computer to the mains. I had a copy of my plan for the session in front of me on the lectern so I continued as if this was no big deal. The MC hurried to the back of the room to find the technician and a power cord. I just kept going until the computer was connected and the PowerPoint came back on.

Odd that the conference organiser had not checked the equipment. I got in early to make sure the projector, computer and PowerPoint worked.

Next time I will look under the lectern to make sure the computer is charging and not running on the battery.

2. **Sickness.**

Maybe you wake up feeling unwell or feel incapable of continuing doing your presentation.

What to do?

Decide quickly whether you will struggle on or get someone to take your place.

Once when working locally, I was violently ill overnight. Something I ate. I didn't sleep much and kept visiting the toilet. Amazing how the body wants to get rid of something it doesn't like. I was still dizzy in the morning and had trouble standing up without dizzy spells. No chance of doing the presentation.

I had the name of another speaker and friend who was speaking before me and texted her early in the morning. I told her what had happened and suggested I send her my presentation. I was due to start at 10.30am. She agreed to fill in for me. She is a true friend. 'A friend in need ….' I would have done the presentation if I could have stood up. I couldn't so I didn't. The audience got what they wanted. Some contacted me to say thanks for making sure my presentation went ahead without me.

So, what can you do to minimise the chance of feeling unwell?

Mostly this is common sense. Eat your usual meal on the night before and at breakfast. Get enough sleep. See yourself as an athlete preparing for an event. Don't drink alcohol the night before. If the client invites you to dine with them the night before either decline or be very sensible. They may feel you are being unsociable. Imagine how much stronger their reaction will be if you do a bad job at your presentation. Think like an elite athlete. You wouldn't have a late night before an important event.

3. **Difficult audience**.

Have you ever had an individual who clearly didn't want to be present or who was determined to make life difficult for you? Hopefully you have not had a whole audience with this intention.

Earlier I mentioned an occasion when I noticed a participant reading the newspaper in the front row, spread out on his lap. I think I was supposed to notice. I said to him quietly "Seems like you would rather read the paper than listen to me". He replied, not so quietly "You are a @#$%& genius." I think he was being sarcastic. He told me later he had been told to attend. He said he hadn't been told to listen. I would probably have reacted poorly if I was forced to attend a conference when I was very busy at work.

Ask the organiser about individuals or the audience well before your presentation. What sort of an audience are they? Is there anyone in the audience I should know about? Ask about the prevailing mood.

Ask about sensitive topics e.g. redundancies, organisational change. I was once warned about a senior manager who would intervene if I did not use female pronouns. I stuck to the plural as I have done in this book. Another time, I was asked to avoid using the word God. You know, stuff like OMG. I don't anyway but it was good to be prepared and avoid offending anyone.

Have a plan for dealing with difficult individuals. Don't defend yourself. Be honest. 'I was not told about any salary freeze'. Be prepared to say 'I don't know'. Validate rather than reject how they are feeling. "I am sorry that you have been asked to attend against your will during your last week at work." Can I do anything to make this easier for you?'

A simple model for answering questions looks like this…

You get a question, maybe a tricky one...

1. Thank you for the question
2. Paraphrase – 'So you want to know….?'
3. Answer the question if you can or postpone answering.
4. Check that the questioner is happy with your response or postponement (during the break)
5. Ask 'Are there any more questions?'

If you respond with "I don't know the answer to that question" and they say "you should know. "Just say "You are right." I will find out the answer and contact you'.

Don't start a debate on whether you should know the answer to every question.

Don't get drawn into office politics. You will end up between a rock and another rock. You will lose.

Often the lead in is something like "What is your opinion about hiring family members? Do you think husbands and wives should work in the same team?" "What do you think about our office design?" Beware. You may get away with reversing the question. "What do YOU think about hiring family members?"

Either ask "Why do you need to know my opinion" or avoid the question . Maybe say " I don't have an opinion" or "I don't think my opinion is relevant to what we are doing today."

4. Working for someone with a big ego.

A person with a big ego knows everything. Wants to control everything. Micromanages you. Insists on knowing what you are going to say in advance. Tells you not to mention certain topics.

I'll give you an example.

I was the MC at a conference for a large organisation. The CEO had written the introductions for all the speakers and told me to read them exactly as they were written.

In one of the breaks he handed me a note and asked me to read it to the audience. It was a supposedly funny comment about one of the senior managers who was in attendance. I had not met him. If I had been the senior manager I would have been offended or annoyed at what I was supposed to read to the audience. I told the CEO that I was uncomfortable reading the note and suggested he read it himself. He assured me that the person would not take offence. I told him I was still uncomfortable to make comments which sounded critical or unkind. He told me that If I didn't read it, I wouldn't work for him again. I have not worked for him again. I prefer to work with people not for people and I am not going to get cheap laughs at the expense of a stranger in the audience.

Humour is meant to create an atmosphere of enjoyment. If someone is going to look foolish to get a laugh, I make sure it is me. I tend not to take myself seriously. My work, I take very seriously. I am not the message. I am the messenger. The message is important.

Another time, the CEO said he would stand at the back or the room and wave his hands when I had five minutes to go. I did have my own watch.

It's your call in how far you can go with a person with a big ego. Careful you don't compete with them. If they are in a senior position, you lose. If you can do what they want without compromising your values, then do it. If you can't, don't.

You can keep your own ego under control by being curious instead of knowing everything, being humble instead of boasting and telling the truth instead of exaggerating.

Like Nadal and Federer. They both let their behaviour do the talking.

Mostly things have worked fine for me over my speaking career. The equipment mostly works. The person hiring me is usually great to work with. My health has been exceptionally good. You get the picture.

Be prepared in advance.

The night before, create a checklist like when you travel overseas. Pack your bag the night before. Put your equipment in the car the night before if you are driving yourself. Less chance that you will dash out and forget it. Tick off everything that you will need for your presentation. Do a pre mortem. Do it when you are calm.

So next time you present, what can you do to manage the risk?

What will you do if…?

Your computer won't work.

The projector won't work.

You feel unwell on the morning of the presentation.

There is a very grumpy, disruptive cynic in the audience.

You have an unco-operative audience.

You are being pushed around by a very controlling organiser.

The wrong PowerPoint presentation is on screen in the room you are speaking in.

The CEO of the organisation you are working for steals your time. They want to 'say a few words before you start'. CEOs don't say a few words…. ever.

There is a fire alarm in the middle of your presentation.

You turn up to the wrong venue.

An expletive pops out of your mouth from nowhere.

What would your Plan B look like for any of these situations?

Always have a Plan B.

Expect the best and be ready for the worst.

If you are wondering what I did when the power failed and the audience were plunged into darkness.

I paused and then said "It looks like we have a temporary problem with the power supply. Maybe the bill wasn't paid on time. Feel free to talk amongst yourselves until the supply is back on again."

They did talk amongst themselves and the power did come on soon afterwards. I believe that my remaining calm helped the situation.

Always have a Plan B. Always.

12. Hit the road

Now what?

Imagine you have a high performance, expensive car. Four-wheel drive with all the safety features. But…. you want to save money on tyres. You buy cheap tyres that are meant to last a long time. They don't grip so well but should last forever. Better quality tyres are expensive and don't last as long because they grip better and wear out quicker.

Oddly, the critical part of the car is where it meets the road. A powerful car and cheap tyres are a dangerous combination. You save money, but may lose your life.

My point is that you have done the work and now need to apply what you have learned. You need to hit the road of speaking. It is essential that you practise and do it soon. In my analogy, cheap tyres are the same as neglecting to practise your speaking skills. You do all the hard work but don't see the need to practise to make your skills second nature.

So now what?

You have information on how to design and deliver a presentation. You know how to make your information memorable. You can handle questions. You are using good pictures maybe even Pecha Kucha. You have a Plan B in case anything goes wrong. You have become a student of mindfulness and know how to stay calm and focused. You can remain calm in most situations and don't get stopped by 'nerves'.

Good progress.

Often the problem is not what you know or don't know. It is what you do with what you know. Good intentions are fine when combined with action. There comes a time when you need to take action if you want to improve. Getting more information is sometimes a way of avoiding action. How many times have you taken notes at a seminar and not looked at the notes afterwards?

Taking notes feels like you are making progress or doing something. It isn't.

Watching other speakers does not improve your speaking ability. They are doing. You are watching. Watching doesn't improve doing.

It's time to start practising. You need to find or create opportunities. You need to develop skills and this only comes with practice. Most people don't like public speaking so you won't have much competition. Remember that the ones that won't volunteer may still feel the need to criticise your presentation afterwards. Their feedback may be helpful although they can't present themselves. Take their feedback at face value. Feedback is a gift whatever the source. You will know whether their intention is to help you or big note themselves. It may be both.

Let's identify some opportunities for you to present.

I suspect that many times when you speak one to one, you could make the conversation more of a presentation. You could use your laptop with some pictures. I remember asking a specialist about a health concern I had. He pulled out his iPad and showed me several pictures. He used a stylus to add to the pictures and diagrams. He turned a Q & A session into a very informative presentation. Maybe he guessed that I understand much better with visual support, any visual support.

Here are other examples of situations that offer the opportunity to present professionally.

Staff meetings.

Tool box meetings

People leaving the organization.

Welcoming new staff.

Births, deaths, marriages, divorces.

Staff training.

Introducing speakers.

Book clubs.

Family occasions

You can make these presentations more interesting by giving them a title.

Something like….

I am calling today's presentation 'The Spirit of Ubuntu'. Let me explain what Ubuntu means.

Or 'The Gap'. You will have noticed Joan's headstone and that there is gap between 1944 -

2014. Let me tell you what happened during this gap.

I am sure you have read boring titles to courses and seminars. An unimaginative title like:

'Implications for measuring OHS performance and managing OHS risk in today's market.' With a title like this you may not get your audience excited enough to sign up or turn up.

I did attend a presentation called 'Kangaroos don't walk backwards.' Another called 'Jet planes don't have rear view mirrors.'

So, choose a title that creates interest or arouses curiosity. 'How to do something' can get people's attention.

For example:

How to live longer

How to live to 100

How to balance your energy

How to get out of debt quickly

How to avoid stress

How to live with fear

Give thought to your title. You have probably attended movies based on the title and avoided others.

If you do well as a speaker in your team, you may be asked to speak at …

Departmental meetings

State Conferences

National Conferences

International Conferences

Virtual Conferences

If these seem too big for your present view of your ability, contact me and we will stretch your view to include these. Careful you don't restrict your vision with a false view of your capability. I remember working with a young man who was a baker in a country town. I later heard he was speaking at a franchising conference in the USA. He didn't hold himself back with a small vision.

Be ready anytime to give a brief presentation or talk. Push yourself a little. Start out by saying "There are three things we will miss now that …

is leaving." Try this even if you don't know what the three things are. If you don't get to three, ask the audience "What do you think the last one is?" They will help you. Be brave. Don't let fear take away your voice, goals or resolve. The fear of public speaking is not a real fear. What I mean is that the likelihood of the consequences actually happening only exist in your mind.

"What happens if my mind freezes and I don't know what to say?"

"What if I make a fool of myself?"

"What if I am overcome with nerves?"

"What if … what if?"

You can let questions, like thoughts, drift by without engagement. You don't need to answer them. Just say to yourself "There's that question again." Weird how it keeps coming back like a boomerang or sushi train.

Imagine that your CEO asks, "Does anyone have anything to say about our plans for next year?" Many people will have something to say but won't. Fear prevents many people and organisations from improving. It can make cowards of us all. It is not a worthy source of motivation. Once the source of the fear is identified, motivation can come alive. Courage is simply acting while the fear remains. Courage needs fear to be courage. It's hardly courage if there is no fear.

So, your CEO asks "Does anyone want to say anything?"

You rise to your feet. Your voice comes out strong and connected. You say what everyone is feeling with emotion and conviction.

The CEO steps back.

Everyone in the room claps. Some stand up. The rest follow the lead and rise to their feet.

You have found your voice! You have shown your leadership ability by saying what many are feeling but are too fearful to say. You are speaking on their behalf. You have become their leader.

It is important that you become a better speaker and presenter. It is important for your career and personal development. It is important for your organisation's continuing success.

Your confidence will increase as you improve. This confidence will spill into everything you do. No one is confident at the start. If you act as if you are confident, then confidence comes. You don't have to be confident at the start. You just need to appear confident. In fact, if you really focus on what you are doing, there is no time for thinking about whether you are confident or not.

The alternative to speaking out is to take your opinions and good ideas with you to the grave. You can make a difference by speaking out. People will congratulate you "I loved what you said. I wish I had the confidence to speak like you." They may even undervalue your courage and hard work by saying "You are a natural speaker." Just say "Thank You."

You may spend many hours preparing for a brief presentation. Do the work if you want the results. Don't tell anyone how much work you have done. The people who 'wing it' don't feel the need to prepare. It usually shows in their presentations. Do the work. Get the results and the recognition.

Does anyone care how many times an athlete or sportsperson has practised a particular skill if they execute it skillfully?

Do you remember the match winning drop goal by Jonny Wilkinson? Wilkinson played for England in the 2003 World Cup Final against Australia. With one minute to go in the final, Wilkinson stayed back ready for a final attempt at a field goal. With seconds left on the clock, an English player threw a long pass back to Wilkinson who slotted the ball between the posts, winning the Rugby World Cup. Was anyone interested in how many times he had practised this attempt?

Commit to a plan now. Decide on your next presentation. Arrange it. Prepare for it. Design it. Create interesting visuals. Maybe include music. Include some humour.

Think of opportunities coming up in the near future. Someone needs to speak. Why not you?

If you have no opportunities coming up in future, create some. Ask your manager if you can do a presentation on the new product, structure or policy. If you have team meetings and they are very casual, make these meetings interesting with a more formal format and the use of visuals. If you belong to a club, do a presentation on your feet instead of just speaking seated. Start with a story. "Just recently, someone asked me a very challenging question. A question that stopped me in my tracks…."

Your organisation may be interested in online conferencing to save travel costs. This is a great opportunity for you to become familiar with this medium. During lockdown, this method of presenting has become very popular by necessity. Virtual presentations are likely to continue after COVID 19. You will need to develop your style to fit the technology. As with radio and studio recording, you need to increase your projection and energy. You will sound loud and theatrical to yourself but interesting to your audience.

If you have heard people interviewed on the radio, you will know what a mismatch sounds like. An animated, energetic interviewer and a timid, softly spoken, nervous caller. Unfair match. Game over.

If you want support at your place of work, form a speaker's group where you can help each other and give valuable feedback

Go back over this book more than once and work on a specific area until you are happy with your level of skill.

Work on –

Your exciting opening

Your cleverly chunked middle

Your satisfying close

Being very calm – living with fear

Impromptu speaking

Avoiding the common five mistakes

Creating captivating visuals

Mindful listening

Your view of yourself as a presenter (stop criticising yourself)

Your creative use of pictures, photos, visuals

Your ability to tell compelling stories.

Make public speaking one of your signature strengths. You won't have much opposition or competition. Remember that many, many misguided people fear speaking more than death. This means that there are more opportunities for those of us who see the value of speaking as a way of making a difference.

I did warn you that you will get unwanted advice or feedback from people who would never speak themselves. Accept it gracefully. They took the trouble to speak to you in person instead of writing it on a feedback sheet. Show that you are interested by saying "Is there anything else you noticed about my presentation?"

Imagine making a good living from doing something you enjoy. You can as an accomplished speaker even if it is only a small part of your job. If fear is all that is holding you back, be grateful that you don't have far to go to be a success. Especially since this fear is based on a misunderstanding of reality. This fear is really Fake News. It is the same as flying. Flying is very safe. The taxi ride to the airport is much more dangerous. You should be relieved when you get on the airplane and very relieved as it takes off.

As far as I know, no one has ever died from public speaking. They say they died on stage. We know they are exaggerating. Scared maybe. Dying not.

I remember one speaker asking an audience "Who has a fear of public speaking?" One hand went up. He asked the person "Who do you focus on when you are speaking?" "Myself" said the person. "Simple solution" said the speaker. "Focus on your audience instead!" Maybe it is not so simple but you get the point. Think about them and their needs.

Start small with a short presentation to a small group. Keep going as your confidence grows.

You are important. Your message is more important.

Think now about opportunities that you can create to practise your presenting and speaking skills.

What is your message?

Which audience would benefit from hearing your message?

Is there a meeting coming up where you could present information that is of value to the group?

Is there a regular meeting where you could do a slightly more formal presentation rather than just speaking from your place at the table?

Does your organisation make presentations to clients and could you help with these?

Could you offer to help someone else prepare a presentation?

If you make regular reports at a monthly meeting, could you do this in a different or more memorable way?

If you are already a competent presenter, how could you move to the next level?

What could you include to make your presentations more effective?

Don't wait for opportunities to knock on your door. If we stretch this metaphor, maybe opportunities don't knock on doors but wait for someone to come to their door. Maybe they don't knock and are available everywhere, all the time. You need to look for them. They don't look for you. Wouldn't it be a pity if you are waiting for someone to ask you to do a presentation and it never happens. They didn't know that you were interested…because you didn't tell them. Someone else was sent interstate or overseas to speak at a conference on a topic that you know a lot about. Pity.

You need to identify your own opportunities and ask. If you get a 'no', ask why? Ask what you need to do to be considered for speaking and presenting opportunities within your organisation. Keep getting better and keep asking.

Just do it. You know enough. You have a story to tell. You have information that others need to hear. Start doing. Hit the road.

Find your voice. Use it.

Malala Yousafzai found hers. She has even returned to Pakistan where she was shot. She is determined to speak out even if it means that her life is at risk.

Find your voice and use it.

13. Dessert

Mostly, the meal is prepared. Now for the dessert. Not an afterthought but an important part of a meal. I am stretching the comparison of preparing a meal to preparing a presentation.

This chapter is about the small things that need to be considered to make the presentation a resounding success. I assume that the chef will do a quick check of the meals before they are sent out to be eaten by hungry patrons.

Here is a list of small but important items. Finishing touches.

Using the microphone

Dress code

Writing an introduction

Humour

Deciding who is your client

Political correctness and respect

Defining success

Linking with other speakers

Keeping your feet on the ground

I'll cover these briefly.

Using the microphone.

Don't unless you have to. The size of the room and acoustics will dictate the need to use a microphone. If you can be heard without it by simply projecting more, don't use it. It is just more technology that might misbehave. Maybe you have a soft voice.

If you do need to use a microphone, ask for a lapel microphone instead of the lectern microphone. The lectern mike keeps you at the lectern and also forces you to face the mike at all times. The lapel mike is designed to clip onto a tie or blouse just beneath your mouth for best results. If you wear it to one side, the volume will vary as you move your head. It is not really a lapel mike at all. It's really a tie or blouse mike.

Make sure you can clip the mike onto something beneath your mouth just near your throat. This can be awkward for a woman. A necklace can also rub against the mike and create distracting noises. Wear something that allows you to clip the mike close to your throat in the middle of your chest.

The third alternative is a hand-held mike which will restrict your hand movements and will cover part of your face and hide your facial expressions. You need to hold it close to your mouth and this covers your mouth and your smile.

Go for the lapel mike every time.

I always ask for a lapel mike and most people will provide one.

Dress code.

Dress one notch up or down from your audience. Not two or three. Just one. You need to look like the speaker rather than an audience member. If someone came looking for the speaker in a break, make sure they can find you from your appearance. Don't blend in entirely.

You want to look like you put some thought into your appearance especially your shoes.

I am sure you have seen people who have dressed way over the top and look like show ponies. Others look like they slept in their clothes. Somewhere in the middle is best.

Ideally, the audience won't be distracted by your appearance but will get a positive impression. You look like you put serious thought into your appearance. You showed respect to your audience with your choice of clothes.

I have a friend who was asked to speak to a group in Europe. He bought a new suit, shirt and shoes for the occasion. Italian shoes.

Writing an introduction.

Write your own introduction and send it to the person who will be introducing you at least a week before your presentation. Ask them to stick to what you have written.

The introduction is really your launch. It establishes you as knowing what you are speaking about. Maybe you want to be seen as an expert. At the very least, you want to be seen as someone worth listening to. Make the introduction short and to the point. This is not your CV unless you want to speak to a sleeping audience.

I usually send my introduction to the MC for a conference. One MC asked me if it was OK to ask me several questions instead of reading my introduction. The questions had little to do with my presentation and would have used up valuable time. I suggested that we stick to my introduction. I think he wanted to be more than just an MC.

You can be immodest in your introduction as the audience won't know that you wrote it. "We are very fortunate to have............speaking to us today. They have spoken overseas in seven countries and have written a book on the topic". Make sure everything you write is true. Don't count Tasmania as an overseas country. It is part of Australia.

You could include humour. For example, you could say that our speaker today has spoken at conferences in Melbourne, Sydney and...... (mention a very small town as the third). Always gets a laugh. Make sure that no one from this very small town is present. You will know the right town for your audience.

You can follow the introduction with self-deprecating humour.

"Wow. I must get you to do all my introductions. I can't wait to hear myself.'

The alternative is to let the introducer make up their own introduction or take something from your website. This is very risky.

Humour.

I am sure you have heard that humour is not necessary unless you want them to remember your message.

Humour can be kind or very unkind. The best kind is kind.

If you are going to take someone down for laugh, make sure it is you. "Some people think I am pedantic but I am not sure that is the right word."

I could write a book on humour and may still do so.

Discover what style suits you. Don't tell jokes you got from a book. You are not a comedian. You are using humour to reinforce your message or create gaps in the presentation.

The easiest way to get started is to tell stories about what has happened to you in the past. Real stories.

For example, I sometimes get called Bruce. My name is Paddy Spruce. Can you hear a Bruce in there? I also get calls in the evening which start like this "Good morning Mate!" Have you had these calls? Finally, I read a comment from the Organised Crime department of the Police Force. Is there a department for disorganised crime? Would they answer the phone?

Humour happens around us all the time. You just need to be open, aware and in the mood. You will miss the humour if you are stressed. I remember being asked in a Bank if someone was looking after me... at my age. I was also asked at the same Bank if I wanted a housing loan when I made a small deposit. I did feel the urge to say "Yes, why not?" Don't you see the funny side when asked if someone is serving you and you are the only person in the shop and they are the only person serving.

Finally, make sure your humour comes from the adult you and not the adolescent you. Grown up, clever humour enhances your presentation. No one gets laughed at except you. You use your intelligence. I am not sure why it seems funny when others experience misfortune. Is this schadenfreude or just being adolescent?

I told you I remembered seeing a speaker trip when going up the stairs to the lectern. He fell and dropped his notes. It seemed funny for a moment and then tragic and back to funny when he jumped to his feet and said "Gotcha didn't I?" We laughed to relieve the stress caused by his accident. For some reason, this sudden, unexpected change caused people to laugh.

Well-spaced humour breaks your presentation into bite sized pieces and gets people to breathe in more deeply.

Grown up humour is best for grownups. Your sense of humour needs to mature as you do.

Who is my client?

Seems like an obvious question. Is it the audience? Is it the person who hired you or asked you to speak? Is it the person who has the problem? Maybe it's the HR Manager or the CEO. Maybe the CFO.

Let's say you are asked to speak to a team whose morale is a little low. You are asked by a manager to speak to this team to lift their spirits. They feel that the team seems down and it is affecting their performance.

You haven't spoken to the team leader or Training Manager.

What if the Manager wants you to tell them how well off they are? Tell them they at least have a job. Tell them they could be unemployed and should be grateful for the generous salaries and excellent working conditions.

You see my point.

You need to decide who your client is. This person needs to be at least satisfied with your presentation. Sometimes this person doesn't mind if the audience don't like your presentation as long as their performance improves.

Political Correctness and Respect.

You know what this is so I won't say much. Suffice to say that you must not upset anyone in the audience by reference to minorities or any of the isms. Sexism, ageism, racism. Be very careful around Religion. You can mention cynicism. Offend no one. Also mind your language. Some swearing has always existed but it seems to be entering the mainstream through television and the movies. Some word bombs are still not acceptable mainstream. Bombs explode.

I recently heard a speaker drop the F bomb and suddenly realise that the session was being recorded. He stopped and asked if the bomb could be deleted.

Set your own standards high. Stretch your vocab without resort to swearing. I worked at one place where the F bomb was replaced with flop and flopping. There are plenty of other English words to use. It gets boring when the same adjective is used to describe everything. Imagine saying that everything is awesome. Awful used to mean full of awe but got overused and dumped. Awesome will also die from overuse. I hope.

All of these words have changed their meaning because of overuse:

Awful, Nice, Silly, Naughty, Cool, Hussy, Wicked.

Only say things about public figures that you would be comfortable having these public figures say about you, in public. Only say about them what you would say if they were present.

Don't use shock tactics to keep your audience engaged. You may keep them awake but also alienate them.

Political correctness keeps changing. Stay in the middle of this change. Don't be a leader in exploring the boundaries. Don't be the last person to make the change.

When you speak to anyone you are developing a habit. If there is language you don't want to use in front of an audience, don't use it anywhere. It might pop out under pressure. I have seen speakers trip on the way to the podium and let out an expletive.

Umms and Ahaas aren't really included in political correctness but will annoy or distract.

These are really fillers for gaps in your presentation. Your mind suddenly hears a gap and plugs the hole. It would be much better to leave the hole empty. Stay silent.

Instead of "My name is umm Peter or Angela." You could say "My name is………. Peter." The pause will create interest.

PC keeps changing. Make sure you are too. Show respect.

Defining success.

Do you or your audience decide that your presentation was a success?

What if you did an average job with no preparation and they liked the presentation? Or the reverse. You worked very hard and did everything you were asked to do and they didn't like your presentation?

My suggestion is that you define your own success. You know your purpose. If you achieved it, the presentation was a success.

You may think you did an excellent job but get feedback a week later that someone didn't like your presentation or took offence to a comment you made. You don't know who made the complaint or which comment was considered offensive.

If you did your best on the day, be pleased with yourself. Take any feedback onboard and make improvements but be proud that you did your best.

Some audience members will never acknowledge that you did a good job.

Some years ago I spoke at a conference and was sent the feedback at week later. One person wrote "Male pronouns". I am not sure what to do with this feedback except to acknowledge that they went to the trouble of giving me some feedback. It was made anonymously so I can't question the feedback. In fact, I thought I was pronoun neutral. I tried harder after this.

Be careful about giving feedback to others. Don't ask them to change things they can't. If your purpose is to help them get better, be specific. If your purpose is to get even, keep the feedback to yourself. Have you ever been criticised for your age, race, gender, height, nationality or accent? I can't change any of these and don't have an accent anyway. I understand that Australians are the only people on earth who don't have an accent. Amazing, eh?

Success is ongoing. We know of people who have been defined as a success after one event or a failure after one event. Success is not a noun in speaking. It is a verb. A doing word.

If the audience is asked for written or online feedback, make sure you assess your own performance first before being coloured by the audience's view. I suggest that you wait for the next day to look at the audience's feedback.

Define your own success. Keep improving. Every presentation needs to be better than the last one. You are only as good as your last presentation.

Linking with other speakers.

Let's say that you are not the only speaker at an event. It is important that you support and link up with the other speakers. To do this, you will need to hear the other speakers.

I suggest that you arrive early enough to hear everyone before you so you can refer to what they say and link it with your message. Be generous in your comments about the other speakers. "I agree entirely with what……said earlier this morning".

Of course, I am assuming that you do agree with what the other speakers said. If you don't, don't try to score points by disagreeing with them in detail. At best, you might say, if asked "I have a different opinion on that topic".

If you support and link with other speakers, they may do the same for you. Be generous.

Make speaking a life time profession. Be prepared to meet the same people you met on the way up, on the way down.

You could become a keynote speaker in your own aged care facility. Maybe you can get some other speakers to join so you are not the only one.

Keeping your feet on the ground.

Now what does this mean?

It means not drifting into the clouds and believing all your own marketing material.

Speaking can be seductive. You might begin to believe that you are superior to your audience members. You know more so you believe you are more. It can happen.

You might start to boast a little in your presentations. You might get a little defensive when given constructive feedback. You might bend the truth. You say it happened to you but it didn't.

A lot of people have said that they have thrown a lone starfish back into the ocean. I was tempted once. To tell the story, I mean. I have no desire to throw starfish back into the ocean. They may be resting on the sand with no desire to be thrown back by some do gooder.

You say you have spoken overseas…in Tasmania.

You are an author…of an eBook.

You earn a six-figure income. Is the first figure a nought?

You might like to make comparisons between yourself and other speakers. "I would never give the advice they gave you." The best comparison is between you now and you then.

If your ego gets larger, your impact on your audiences will get smaller. They might turn off and no longer listen to you. Glazed eyes are an indication that they have gone out and left the lights on. Einstein said that the greater the knowledge the smaller the ego and vice versa.

Remember that you are not the message. You are simply the messenger. It doesn't matter how they get the message as long as they get the message. Your message matters more than you do. Your message will last longer than you by a long shot. We are still quoting the ancient

Greeks even if we don't know which ancient Greek we are quoting.

The best way to keep yourself grounded is to practise:

Humility. Acknowledge the help you get from others and how little you can achieve on your own. Read about Ubuntu.

Truthfulness. Only speak the truth as you know it. Don't stretch the truth. Do it enough and your truth becomes THE truth, in your mind. The truth is not elastic.

Curiosity. Be very interested to learn more. Assume that you will always be learning. You will never peak as a speaker or a learner. There will always be room for improvement.

If you really focus on what you are doing, you won't have the computing power to maintain your ego. Your ego won't exist. You will be totally absorbed in your presentation. You won't have the extra computing power to think about being superior.

Here is quick summary of the small things that can have a large impact.

- Don't use a mike unless you have to
- Dress to compliment your audience
- Write your own introduction
- Use the right kind of humour – kind humour
- Keep your client happy – the real client
- PC or not PC, that is the question?
- Define your own success
- Honour your tribe – other speakers and presenters
- Stay grounded - don't believe all the feedback you get
- Feedback is neither good nor bad. It is just feedback.
- Be prepared to meet the same people you met on the way up, on the way down. Pay your dues.
- And finally, if there is a technician in the room assisting you, make sure you get to meet them and become their friend in a short time. Sometimes, they leave the room. Make sure you know how to contact them when they do.
Acknowledge them in your presentation.

Now you are ready to serve the meal. Bon appetit! Make a difference.

14. Personality and other excuses.

Have you ever used your personality as an excuse?

Maybe "I am an introvert and find it difficult to speak to an audience of more than one." "I need to prepare for months to do a good job when I do presenting." "I don't stick around after a presentation as I am tired and need to recharge on my own.I don't like small talk anyway."

Or "I enjoy sharing personal information with my audiences". "I don't need to prepare much for a presentation." "I like to stick around afterwards as I feel energised by the discussions that follow." "I enjoy public speaking."

Personality is different from temperament and shy is different from introverted.

We are born with a temperament. Our personality develops and can change during our lifetime. Sometimes it doesn't. I am an extrovert according to Myers-Briggs but display many traits of an introvert. I get energised after a speaking engagement by being alone. I usually think before I speak. I dread sitting beside someone on a long flight who wants to do small talk. I would rather read. I take a little while to be comfortable with people and then speak freely and personally but I am selective. I have learned to behave like an extrovert when speaking to larger groups but find it tiring. I only notice this when I have finished.

I only mention this because it will have an effect on your speaking ability and will give you a sense of how hard it may be for you to become a professional presenter and speaker. I am not trying to discourage you but rather getting you prepared for hard work.

Do you prefer one on one conversations to group activities?

Are you a good listener?

Do you think before you speak?

If you are asked to do a presentation, would you prefer to prepare on your own or seek the help of others?

If you answered 'Yes' to these questions, you are likely an introvert or leaning to that side of the continuum.

Teamwork is very popular at the moment and brainstorming is considered an essential step when solving problems in a group. Brainstorming suits extroverts. They get energised by the input of others. It prompts them to dig deeper. It can have the opposite effect on introverts. They start deep. They can come up with more ideas on their own.

So, as an introvert, you may find it difficult to speak to a large audience and will need to prepare your content and your delivery well in advance. Impromptu speaking may be difficult for you. It may be difficult but not impossible. You may only want to speak on topics that you know about and will want to know who is in the audience. You will stick to time and want to be given your full allotted time. You may find it stressful to be suddenly given more or less time. You will want to clarify questions from the audience before answering. You may not want questions during your presentation. You will need to warm up.

As an extrovert, you may prefer a larger audience to a smaller one. You may not need much preparation and impromptu speaking is seen as a challenge rather than a problem. You wouldn't think it too difficult to be asked to speak at a meeting with little notice. You can adjust your preparation along the way and could cope with more or less time at the last moment. You can deal with questions during your presentation and don't see them as an interruption.

Now, of course, few people are either completely introverted or extroverted. We are all a blend of both. You may lean in one direction when presenting or speaking. You can also learn how to behave like the other. It won't become second nature but you will be able to do it to the satisfaction of your audience. I am generally quiet at dinner parties unless I sit beside someone interesting. In fact, I could MC a conference as the upbeat energiser and then sit quietly at the dinner in the evening. I will also likely go to bed early to be ready for the next day.

Here is an example from my life.

My wife and I were at a conference and there was a Queensland holiday on offer as a door prize. The winning ticket would be announced at the end to make sure everyone stayed. I don't remember the seat number but my wife and I had consecutive numbers. Let's say 94 & 95.

The MC called out the winning number 94 and it was mine. I paused to think about the implications, whether the airfares were included, when we might go etc. When I didn't react, my wife assumed that it must be the person on her other side so she turned to the person and said "I think you have won the holiday!" He said he "No, I have number 96. It must be the person beside you.". My wife then said to me in a voice that expressed disbelief "Do you have number 94?" You can imagine her surprise when I said "Yes." She couldn't understand why I hadn't reacted by jumping to my feet in excitement, as an extrovert, she would have done.

If you lean towards introversion as a presenter, here is my challenge to you:

Tell inspiring stories

Encourage people to ask questions during your presentation and allow time for these questions

Add more drama and energy to your presenting style

Project your voice more or use a microphone

Add more colour to your visual support

Dress for effect e.g. wear a hi vis vest if you are speaking about safety.

Stick around after your presentation to answer questions

Stretch your areas of expertise

Use your strengths.

Be punctual

Research your material

Learn to manage conflict

Think about how to answer a question before answering

Stick to what you know

If you lean towards extroversion, my challenge is to:

Present in a logical way with strong content that is well researched

Quote your sources

Leave questions until the end or not at all

Dress conservatively – Make your content do the talking

Tone down your volume and energy

Make sure your message is more important than you are

Remember your strengths.

Vary your intensity

And let your passion show

I am certainly not suggesting that introversion is better than extroversion or vice versa. I am simply saying that you need to balance your style to suit your audience. Assume that they are half introverts and half extroverts. Be half and half yourself. Use your natural personality strengths and develop your whole personality.

In my career as a speaker, I have seen many extroverted, motivational speakers who have inspired audiences. As an MC I have heard many introverted topic experts and scientists speak quietly about significant topics. Imagine if they had the strengths of both introverts and extroverts. The motivational style inspires us to make change and take action. The educational style informs us about why we need to change and how to do it in a sustainable way.

Earlier I mentioned temperament as being different from shyness. Temperament is a predisposition from birth. Shyness can be fear based. Introverts don't have to be shy but will be if fear is involved. A person may be sitting alone because they are shy or because they simply prefer sitting alone. The fear can be managed. Introverts generally don't like networking but may have to do it as part of their jobs. They may need to mix with an audience before a presentation. Mindfulness will help with managing the fear associated with networking and presenting. Shyness needs to be seen for what it is. It is really a thought or feeling that is given too much attention. Introversion needs to be recognised and exploited. It can be a huge asset as can extroversion.

I suspect that extroversion has been getting the inside running for at least this century. Character used to be valued highly in the past. Personality became popular from the time of Dale Carnegie. Character was deep inside and quiet. Your behaviour told people about your character usually afterwards. Sometimes posthumously. Personality was obvious and on the surface. First impression. Big smile. Energetic projection. Your stereotypical car salesman. Even some churches have now gone the route of high energy delivery. Some believe that quiet believers are not real believers.

If you are an extrovert you will be in the ascendancy for a while longer as a speaker. Be ready for the change that is coming. If you are an introvert, work hard to release your energy as well as your content. Make your passion more obvious. Share it more generously despite feeling awkward. People sometimes look for speakers who entertain rather than inform. They may have a sprinkling of entertaining speakers during a conference. These people will be extroverts or introverts who have learned to speak like extroverts. Surprisingly, many comedians are introverts who know how to act. You hardly recognise them off stage. If you want to annoy them ask them to say something funny. Like most introverts, they are scripted on stage. Rarely, like Robin Williams, they are unscripted and unplugged.

There is a time for an extroverted, inspirational, motivational presentation. There is also a time for a content rich presentation that genuinely educates your audience. Sometimes there is a time for both within the same presentation.

If you find it difficult to develop your personality and feel very awkward when behaving outside your usual boundaries, practise until you can almost feel comfortable. It's a lot like stretching muscles or learning a new language or getting used to new technology. You will return to your comfortable personality after the stretch. I prefer to be alone after a presentation to debrief and recharge. Some speakers want to kick on with members of the audience.

I have known many speakers who want to be left alone to prepare and also prefer to be alone afterwards to recharge. I used to work with a presenter who always went for a long walk after a training session or presentation. I am sure you won't be surprised to hear that many speakers and actors are introverts who have learned to behave like extroverts because it enhances their delivery and performance…and job prospects.

So, my suggestion is….

Recognise your preferred resting personality. Do you like to be alone or with others when you have finished presenting? Do you feel under or overwhelmed by the response of an audience? Do you prefer to prepare with a group or on your own? Can you pause when asked a question or do you answer immediately? What's your first impulse?

For the next week, I suggest that you practise behaving outside your usual range of personality. Do more of what you usually don't do much of.

If you are introverted…

Project more. It will seem loud to you at first.

Start with a story.

Try pecha kucha.

Improvise. Depart from your script occasionally

Let your voice speak louder than your content

Share your passion – crank up your energy. (It will sound theatrical to you)

If you are extroverted…

Plan your next presentation to the minute

Work with a script and stick to the script

Disclose your sources

Let your content speak louder than your voice.

Pull back your energy occasionally

Put pauses in your presentation

You were born with a temperament. Your personality developed with new experiences. You likely have a home base that you return to for recovery. Don't live there all the time. Just go there to recover.

Don't use your personality as an excuse. Expand it.

15. Next Level.

Let's just say that you do everything I suggest and practise until you become a polished speaker. You use mindfulness to help you manage your thoughts and nervous energy. The obvious question now is how do you move to the next level? How do you do more speaking or do it better? If you want to get paid, how can you get paid more? What is the next level?

If you were doing martial arts, you would go for a grading and move to the next level. Sixth or seventh kyu. Academically, you would move from a graduate degree to a masters or further. Nursing Div 2 to Div 1.

Speaking?

First, be sure you know why you want to move to another level. What I mean here is, ask yourself if you are content to keeping speaking occasionally to your work colleagues but do it better. The next level might simply be to improve rather than move to another audience or get paid to speak. Speaking is seductive. You can get tricked into believing that you have become a more important person just because you are speaking more often to larger groups.

Your importance won't change whatever you do. You will always be important but never more important than anyone else despite what they do for a living. Doctors don't trump cleaners in the importance stakes. Income sure but importance never.

So, decide on whether you just want to keep improving in your current situation or consider changing your situation.

I have met many people who speak occasionally and get inspired by hearing a professional speaker who is highly regarded or well paid. They get carried away with the dream and are often disenchanted with their current situation. They want speaking to take them away from the humdrum of their present situation. Beware. You may be creating an ideal profession in your mind just because you are unhappy with your present job. I am not suggesting that you don't change but just want you to make sure you are acting for the right reasons so you won't have regrets in the future.

Make sure you are moving towards something exciting or helpful to others not away from what you dislike.

Make sure you are acting towards a goal that will meet your present and likely future needs. It is very risky to move away from a situation just because you are not satisfied. For example, you might see speaking as a way of getting away from an unpleasant situation where there is not enough challenge or your ability is not recognized.

Compare this to having a niggling cold that just won't go away. Eventually, you will do almost anything to get over the illness. You are wide open to exotic cures. Once better, you won't understand why you were so desperate. The same for speaking. It won't solve all your problems. It is a great profession but not an escape.

So, if you decide to take the step of doing more speaking and considering becoming a full-time speaker, make sure you have done your homework as if you were starting a new business. Your current job may be meeting many of your needs and you are taking this for granted. Speaking is exciting but may not meet some of your needs. For example, you may have to travel and miss special occasions at home. If you don't travel a lot and find visiting the airport exciting or if you like staying at a hotel, beware.

We humans can get used to almost anything. The joy doesn't last forever not does the pain. Sometimes the grass is greener somewhere else but you may miss appreciating the grass in your own backyard.

I remember a person falling out of love with his Mercedes days after purchase. Something very small annoyed him and he was thinking about returning it. It looked wonderful to me. His joy didn't last long. It seldom does. Enjoy everything while it lasts.

Believe me it is possible to find travelling a burden and staying at hotels an inconvenience.

There's my warning.

I am not saying that Speaking is something that you will get over soon. It is a skill that you can enjoy all your life. You can also help many people. See it for what it is rather than an escape. Be clear about your purpose and then embrace the challenge.

Now let me make some suggestions for moving to the next level.

Be very clear about why you want to go to the next level

Create a support group

Get a coach

Become a better marketer than a speaker

Have a business plan

Learn to deal with setbacks

Do what it takes – spend on your development

Be very clear why you want to go to the next level

Your purpose is very, very important.

Your purpose is the answer to "Why do you want to do more speaking?"

Be careful if you want to do more speaking to get away from what you are currently doing or doing it to please others or doing it to solve a pressing problem. None of these motives are sustaining in the long term.

If you want to speak more because you really enjoy speaking, find it meaningful and want to benefit others, your motives and energy will last much longer and you will handle setbacks better.

Ideally, you want to improve your speaking to benefit others. You want to help them live a rich, meaningful, stimulating life. You want to help them enjoy their work more. You want their businesses to prosper. If you help others, they will help you. It will seem more authentic if you are coming from the truth yourself. You can speak about enjoying work because you enjoy your work. Make sure you do what you teach.

You also need to be very clear about your values. You need to be able to answer the question "What is important to me?" without a pause.

We all know examples of organisations that say they want to help us when they are really just looking after themselves. Be honest with yourself when deciding on what matters to you.

So next level or just keep improving at the same level?

You decide.

What now?

I suggest that you go over this book again and work on a preparing a presentation using all the information. Choose a topic that you know about and choose an audience who would benefit from your presentation.

Once you have prepared well, look for opportunities to present. Create opportunities. Even if you are one chapter ahead of your audience, you can help them with information or motivation or both.

Find your voice.

Use it to help others.

Maybe that's why you have a voice.

16. Keep Reading.

Here are some good books to keep you going.

The Artistry of Training – Stephanie Burns

Presentationzen by Garr Reynolds

Slide:ology by Nancy Duarte

Resonate by Nancy Duarte

The Confidence Gap by Dr Russ Harris

Presenting to Win by Jerry Weisman

Made to Stick by Chip & Dan Heath

The Happiness Trap by Dr Russ Harris

Wherever you go, there you are by Jon Kabat-Zinn

Mindfulness for Life by Dr Stephen McKenzie & Dr Craig Hassed

Mindfulness – Finding Peace in a Frantic World by Mark Williams

Mindfulness – 24 ways to live in the moment through art- Christophe Andre

Finding your Element by Ken Robinson

Finding Flow by Mihaly Csikszentmihalyi

That Presentation by Conradi and Hali

The Complete Idiot's Guide to Public Speaking by Laurie Rozakis

If you want to chat or get help with improving your speaking skills or finding your voice, contact me.

www.paddyspruce.com.au

0418 996970

email – paddy@paddyspruce.com.au

Find your voice and use it to help others. Speak for those who can't. Get started NOW.

Appendix

Delivery Styles

Which of these seven styles is your preference?

1. Read from notes without looking up at your audience.
2. Read from notes but occasionally look up at your audience.
3. Read from notes but also improvise in between reading your notes.
4. Use bullet points and improvise without notes.
5. Improvise using a mind map or symbols on a page.
6. Improvise using a mental mind map or acronym.
7. Improvise. Speak spontaneously and let your message come out.

All of these styles can be used to convey your message effectively.

Consider widening your range by trying other styles.

Develop a 'radio' voice. Speak as if you are on the radio. Emphasise the important words.

Project as if you need a microphone but don't have one.

Pause before important words.

Let your emotion and personality come out in your voice.

Practise by reading stories to small children.

You've made it if they clap!

Appendix

My Attitude to Public Speaking.

Which of these describe your attitude to public speaking?

1. I really enjoy public speaking and feel relaxed and in control when in front of an audience.
2. I like public speaking but need to manage my nerves. I also like to be given time to prepare.
3. I will accept a request to do public speaking but don't seek opportunities. My attitude is 'I will do it if I have to'. I find it stressful.
4. I don't like public speaking and will avoid it if I can. If I am forced, I will do an acceptable job but will find the preparation and delivery very stressful.
5. I hate public speaking and will avoid it whenever I can. Just thinking about it makes me stressed.

What thoughts do you have about your ability to speak in public?

Do these thoughts hinder your performance or willingness to accept an invitation to speak in public?

How do you manage these thoughts when you are compelled to speak in public?

When you finish a presentation are you relieved or disappointed that it has finished?

Have you tried to change your attitude to public speaking?

What have you tried? Did it work?

What can you do to change your attitude?

One way of changing your attitude is to label the negative thought or feeling when it appears. Say to yourself 'Here's that negative thought or feeling in my stomach'. Just labelling it as a thought or feeling can take away the risk that you are hearing something that is true, factual or accurate.

Imagine that you were on a river cruise in France and woke up with a stiff neck on the day that you were going to visit Avignon. Maybe you had the thought 'It might rain today'. You wouldn't let the stiff neck or the thought about rain stop you from getting off the boat, would you?

You would likely put it aside and enjoy a walk around Avignon.

About the Author

Paddy Spruce is an award-winning conference speaker and public speaking coach. He has spoken at conferences in Europe, Asia, New Zealand and in all Australian States and Territories. He is a former State President of the Professional Speakers Association (Australia).